Anzacs Over England

Anzacs Over England

The Australian Flying Corps
in Gloucestershire
1918–1919

DAVID GOODLAND and ALAN VAUGHAN

ALAN SUTTON

First published in the United Kingdom in 1992
Alan Sutton Publishing Ltd · Phoenix Mill · Far Thrupp
Stroud · Gloucestershire

First published in the United States of America in 1993
Alan Sutton Publishing Inc · 83 Washington Street · Dover NH 03820

British Library Cataloguing in Publication Data

Goodland, David
Anzacs over England
I. Title II. Vaughan, Alan
940.4

ISBN 0-7509-0277-9

Library of Congress Cataloging in Publication Data applied for

Typeset in 12/13 Times.
Typesetting and origination by
Alan Sutton Publishing Limited.
Printed in Great Britain by
The Bath Press, Avon.

For Cheryl, Anna and Brian

Contents

Foreword   ix

Acknowledgements   xiii

Chapter 1: The Arrival of the AFC   1

Chapter 2: Photographic Reconnaissance   11

Chapter 3: Social Intercourse   17

Chapter 4: Three Australian Personalities   56

Chapter 5: Crashes and Casualties   74

Chapter 6: Myths and Legends   87

Chapter 7: The Leighterton Graves   99

Chapter 8: Peace and Repatriation   107

Chapter 9: Left Behind: Men and Memories   121

Chapter 10: The Anzacs' Gloucestershire Diary   131

Australian Flying Corps personnel
buried at Leighterton   140

Foreword

This story begins and ends in the corner of a graveyard in the village of Leighterton in Gloucestershire. There can be found the graves of twenty-five Australian servicemen who died during and after the First World War, killed here in England while learning to handle the early aeroplanes. They belonged to the Australian Flying Corps (AFC).

The part that these twenty-five airmen play in this short history is a sad one, but in remembering their tragic deaths we celebrate their lives. They, and their colleagues who survived, occupied the Stroud district of Gloucestershire for less than eighteen months, yet they are still remembered today.

They were part of the ANZAC (Australian and New Zealand Army Corps) force that took part in the 'Great Australian Adventure', the 'six-bob-a-day tourists' as they laughingly called themselves, who had volunteered to come to Europe and help defend an Empire in distress.

They came from a vast continent still being developed, and found themselves in an English rural backwater which had hardly changed in two hundred years. The First World War, however, changed many things in the British Isles and, in its way, the presence of the Australians helped to speed up that process in this community. As the chairman of Tetbury Urban District Council put it just before they left: 'This old town has much to learn from the young Australians. We depend so much upon precedent and delving into musty documents to find out what happened a century before, while young Australians simply come to a decision on the facts before them.'

In this book we have tried to cover every aspect of the ANZAC invasion of the Cotswolds, from their daredevil antics in the sky to their high-spirited and sometimes awesome behaviour in the towns and villages. Apart from being a fascinating history it reveals an extraordinary clash of cultures between English people and the Colonials from the land of the Southern Cross.

Maj. R.C. Phillips MC DFC, Lt.-Col. Oswald Watt OBE, Legion of Honour, Croix de Guerre, Gen. Birdwood, Commander AIF and Maj. R.S. Brown together in an aircraft hangar at Minchinhampton, 1919

During our researches over the last six years we have made many friends in England and Australia. The archives of Gloucester and Cirencester Libraries, the *Stroud News and Journal*, the *Dursley Gazette* and the Australian War Memorial have been generously placed at our disposal.

Perhaps our most exciting find was the discovery, in Canberra, of a film made at Minchinhampton in 1919. There

Gen. Birdwood preparing for a flight at Minchinhampton with the help of instructor, Capt. Les Holden

on the screen were the very men who, up to that time, we had only read about.

It was our original intention to make a straightforward documentary for television audiences in Australia, in order to plug a small gap in the history of ANZAC. In this we were successful, and many Australians watched *Anzacs over England* on 25 April 1989 and 1990, as part of their Anzac Day viewing.

Response to the film in Australia and interest locally resulted in more background information on the AFC in Leighterton and Minchinhampton coming to light, particularly in the form of old photographs. This has given us the material to produce a book, which is accompanied by a re-edited version of the television documentary containing the film found in Canberra.

Seeing Lt.-Col. Watt and Gen. Birdwood walking among the Australian airmen in the hangars at Minchinhampton, and subsequently climbing aboard an AVRO 504 for a flight over the beautiful Cotswold Hills, gives final and undeniable proof that once there really were Anzacs over England.

David Goodland
Alan Vaughan
Nailsworth
1 July 1992

Acknowledgements

With grateful thanks for the invaluable help many people have given, especially for the use of photographs, documents, information and memories. Including, in alphabetical order:

Ian Afflick (Australian War Memorial Canberra), Don Anderson (Western Front Association), Paul Aston, The Australian High Commission, The Bailey Newspaper Group, Barry Barnes, Howard Beard, Lucille Bell, John Bolt, The Bristol and Gloucestershire Gliding Club, David Browne (The *Gloucester Citizen*), John Chamberlain, Margaret Chivers, Laurie Clarke, The Cotswold Gliding Club, Pam Coursedge (Bruton Knowles Ltd), Laurie Donaldson, Penny Ely (Gloucester Record Office), Pete Fletcher, Ross Forsyth, Pamela Foxwell, Percy Hodges, Alan Hogg, Vic Jefferys, Ros Lane (Gloucester Library), David Lowsley-Williams, Masie Martin, Dennis Mason, Revd Mr Mulholland (Leighterton parish church), Stuart McAlister MBE (RAAF), Jose Nash, Lionel Padin, John H.E. Phillips, Juliette Phillips, Ernie Preston, Ron and Bev (Australia), The Royal British Legion (Dursley Branch), Eunice and Donald Rudge, Susan Smee, Jack Sollars, Derek Sparkes, Mike Tagg (RAF Museum, Hendon), David Taylor, Terry Thomas, Ed Tonks, John Tydeman (BBC), Major Vernon, Di Wall, Gerry Weingarth, John Witchell, Brian Wheeler, Jim Woolley, Glyn Worsnip.

CHAPTER 1

The Arrival of the AFC

Australian Recruitment

There was a period in the history of Stroud when visitors from Australia had an enormous impact which has never been forgotten . . .

Jack Sollars, 7 years old in 1918.

When Great Britain entered the First World War in August 1914 she possessed a mere 150 aircraft and less than 2,000 trained officers and men. By the time the war ended the Royal Air Force consisted of 22,000 military aeroplanes and 300,000 officers and men. At least half of these personnel came from the overseas dominions of the British Empire.

Australians in particular were considered excellent pilots, as a letter from the War Office dated 11 July 1916 to AIF Headquarters emphasizes:

I am commanded by the Army Council to inform you that, owing to the expansion of the Royal Flying Corps, a large number of officer pilots will be required during the ensuing year.

In view of the exceptionally good work which has been done in the Royal Flying Corps by Australian-born officers,

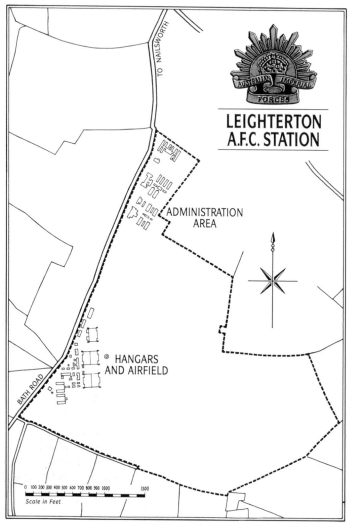

Two maps showing the plan of the completed airfields in 1918. The Leighterton airfield ran parallel to the A46 Bath road and the

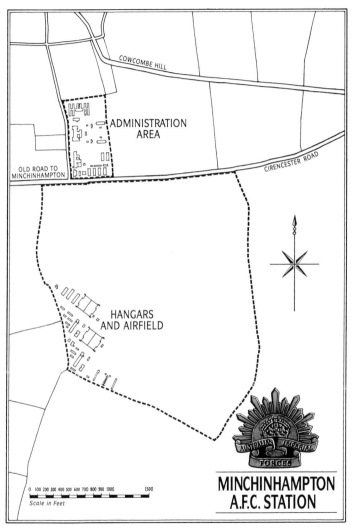

Minchinhampton station was split by the Cirencester road, which was blocked by sightseers on many occasions

Aerial photograph of Leighterton aerodrome, 7 November 1918

An aerial view looking from the south across Leighterton airfield; the Bath road runs from the top right corner of the picture

and the fact that the Australian temperament is specially suited to the flying services, it has been decided to offer 200 commissions in the Special Reserve of the Royal Flying Corps to officers, non-commissioned officers, and men of the Australian Force.

The offer was duly taken up by the Australian Government, but not without reservations. A strong sense of isolation, and the knowledge that in an emergency Australia's own shores would be undefended at this time, led in early 1917 to a joint British/Australian decision to train Australian squadrons in England for service in France and Egypt. The 1st squadron AFC had already seen action in Egypt, and Squadrons 2, 3 and 4 AFC went on to give legendary service in France.

Gloucestershire Invasion

So efficient were these all-Australian squadrons that, by the end of 1917, it was decided to build an AFC training wing consisting of four new squadrons. Squadrons 5, 6, 7 and 8 were to supply replacement pilots to the four squadrons on active service – the average life expectancy of a pilot at the front was then less than three weeks. The headquarters of the new wing, the 1st Wing AFC Training Squadron, was to be in Tetbury, Gloucestershire. The sites chosen for the two aerodromes were a couple of farms near Minchinhampton, called Aston Farm and Down Farm, and a large tract of land near the estate of the Duke of Beaufort at Leighterton.

In the autumn of 1917, local woods were cleared by Canadian foresters to provide timber for the temporary canvas

Part of the Australian 'occupation' force, 1918

and wood (Bessonaux) hangars, which were to be used while the permanent brick hangars were being built.

By the spring of 1918, Minchinhampton (later Aston Down) airfield became the home of the 5th and 6th Training Squadrons of the AFC, and Leighterton housed the 7th and 8th Squadrons AFC. Building work continued at a rapid rate to meet the demands of the cadet pilots, flying instructors, air mechanics and service personnel, who were arriving in the area in great numbers.

Work at the aerodromes immediately brought employment for local tradesmen. The following advert was repeated for several weeks:

WANTED, Immediately,

BRICKLAYERS, CARPENTERS,
PLASTERERS,

For work at
Minchinhampton and Leighterton,
GLOUCESTERSHIRE.

Good Accommodation and Canteen

For Rates of Pay and Free Tickets to
Nailsworth, Mid. Rly., or Badminton,
G.W. Rly., apply nearest Labour Exchange.

Thomas Rowbotham,
Contractor, Birmingham.

The *Gloucester Citizen*, 23 March 1918

*Bessonaux hangars at Minchinhampton aerodrome. The nearest five were
for no. 5 squadron and the other five for no. 6 squadron*

An aerial photograph showing temporary Bessonaux hangars at Leighterton and permanent hangars under construction. No. 7 training squadron is housed in the first five hangars and no. 8 training squadron AFC begins at the sixth hangar.

With hundreds of Australians descending on the area, and the significant change to the environment brought on by the construction at the airfields, local people were clearly aware that the 'invasion' had now turned into an 'occupation'.

The *Stroud Journal* was confused about the identity of the first Australians to fly over Stroud, referring to them incorrectly as the RFC:

LIVELINESS IN THE AIR

Residents from Stroud and the surrounding districts have witnessed several pretty and thrilling aerial sights this week, these being provided by members of the R.F.C. now stationed at an aerodrome in course of erection on the Cotswolds. On Monday about a score of machines, in varying squadrons, crossed our neighbourhood for their objective . . . and thither also arrived on Monday some one hundred and fifty soldiers, chiefly Australians, and, doubtless, very considerably more aerial activity will be seen locally than hitherto.

Stroud Journal, 1 March 1918

One airman went on to give a dazzling aerial display, the first of many to be seen during the next fourteen months. From March 1918 until May 1919, the people of Stroud and all the villages and towns around it were to be made vividly aware of the presence of the 'Aussies'.

CHAPTER 2

Photographic Reconnaissance

*One of my earliest memories is seeing an aerial photograph
of Tetbury, hanging up in the Church School.*
Mr David Taylor (Tetbury resident, son of AFC mechanic)

A large photograph album, presented by the AFC to the
Lowsley-Williams family at Chavenage, contains a wealth of
superb pictures, many of them aerial views of local towns and
villages. The pictures would have been taken on training mis-
sions by pilots practising reconnaissance work. Thought to be
among the first high quality aerial photographs taken of the
area, they are a unique record of a landscape which, up to that
time, had barely changed in 200 years.

Nympsfield in the snow, 1919

Tetbury with the A433 in the foreground. This and the following aerial photographs were taken by the AFC

Tetbury, 27 July 1918 from about 3,000 ft

Westonbirt, 23 June 1918

Charlton village

Horsley village

Leighterton village

Petty France and the Bath road

Gloucester Cathedral, 25 November 1918

Leighterton aerodrome. Permanent hangars under construction, 27 July 1918

CHAPTER 3

Social Intercourse

Sports and Social

They were a very jolly and happy crowd . . .

Lionel Padin (local historian)

From the moment they arrived, the Australians were determined to integrate themselves into the community. Sporting and social activities of all kinds were encouraged. In this atmosphere, friendships flourished and relationships of a more romantic kind developed. With so many young 'diggers' on the loose there might have been considerable friction, but the impression of Lionel Padin, a lad of 10 in 1918, was quite the reverse:

They were a very jolly and happy crowd, very friendly indeed . . . up to all sorts of nonsense . . . like present Australians, very fond of a glass of beer . . . very fond of chatting up the local girls in the village which sometimes of course made problems. One particular lady bore one of the Australian airmen a child and everyone thought that was the end of the affair but she was adamant that her lover would come back from Australia after the war and marry her . . . and sure enough he did.

Five AFC members relaxing after a swim, summer 1918. This cheerful group includes Sgt. Bill Nash, second from the right

Jack Sollars remembers another romantic tale:

One airman was much taken with a young office girl in London Road, Stroud and on several occasions was seen to fly low over the town, at rooftop height and drop *billets doux* to his terrified girlfriend below. The same airman was said to have flown his plane under the railway bridge at Rowcroft, Stroud in an attempt to impress the girl.

The 'Aussies' eventually became famous for their concerts but in the early days it was local ladies in Tetbury and Stroud,

Rowcroft bridge, Stroud: width approximately 21 ft; wingspan of Sopwith Camel 28 ft!

concerned for the comfort of their antipodean visitors, who set out to entertain them. Tea dances, whist drives, social evenings and concerts were organized by special entertainment committees.

The innovations brought by Australians to the area were not confined to their flying activities. The hallowed turf of the Rugby Union ground at Fromehall was the first in the county to accommodate football the Australian way.

There was also the occasion when Horsley village cricket team organized their own version of 'The Ashes'. The result was, not for the first time in the history of Anglo–Australian cricket, very close:

Cricket: Horsley v AFC Leighterton 25th April 1919
On Saturday (25th April 1919) Horsley entertained an XI of the AFC Leighterton. A very pleasant and well contested

19

Miss Grace Street surrounded by antipodean admirers. Miss Street was the daughter of Robert Street, who ran the cycle shop (later a garage, now a supermarket) in Long Street, Tetbury. She helped organize social functions for the AFC. This snap was taken in the back garden of 16 Long Streeet in 1918.

1.

DANCE FOR AUSTRALIAN OFFI-
CERS AND SOLDIERS.—A very en-
joyable dance arranged in honour of the
Australian soldiers stationed at the aero-
drome at Leighterton was held in Messrs
R. A. Lister & Co.'s women's canteen,
Dursley, on Saturday evening. Eight offi-
cers and 80 men made the journey. The
music was supplied in excellent style by
Mr. William Webb's Band, and Mr.
George Lister discharged the duties of
M.C. The arrangements for the event
were very much appreciated by the
Colonials, and were kindly made by Mrs
George Lister, Mrs. Richmond, Mrs. J.
Daniell, and Miss Garside, assisted by
Mrs. J. P. Harding, Mrs. J. W. Cham-
pion, Mrs. H. A. Newth, and Miss Sea-

friends of Aubrey
Fred Wakeham
operative Stores
that he has been
and appointed M
25th Arab Labou
the Tigris. Aft
(India) some time
potamia, and fol
through Bagdad, a
sunstroke and mal
to hospital. After
at a rest camp.
examination decla
join his regiment
and he then acce
mentioned, which
bility, being in c
Arabs, Kurds and

ially-
nbed
:n.—
620

len-
sey,
679

ton
per
ed.

704

The Gloucester Citizen, *25 April 1918*

game ended in a victory for the AFC by a narrow margin of four runs. For the Australians S/M Munro obtained seven wickets for 20 runs while A. Luckett for Horsley obtained seven wickets for 22 runs. Air Mechanic Archer, who was the only batsman to obtain double figures, compiled 15 runs. Scores: AFC 39 Horsley 35.

Stroud Journal, 2 May 1919

These events did much to relieve any tension between local people and the Australians, providing an opportunity to let off steam. Edgar Sollars of Gannicox, Stroud, remembers how, as a youth of 16, he went to Stroud Subscription Rooms to see a boxing display by men of the Minchinhampton 'drome'.

The Australian tug o' war team from Leighterton, who easily beat the Americans and British on 21 September 1918

A scratch Stroud rugby team, 13 April 1918. Many of the players in the match, in aid of Stroud Hospital, were Australians

An excited crowd looking on

*On 22 February 1919 an Australian Trench team beat the Australian
Flying Corps (Leighterton and Minchinhampton) team in a rugby match at
Kingsholm, Gloucester, by fifty points to nil. This is the Flying Corps team*

23

The Australian Trench team

Stenning, the celebrated Australian wing three-quarter, runs through his opponents and scores. In all he scored six tries

Star of the evening was the Welsh flyweight, Jimmy Wilde, who had just won the world title for his weight in a twenty-one-round fight with an American. The famous Jimmy was billed to give a three-round bout with Lt. Matty Smith of the AFC, said to be a 'useful type' in the ring.

The house was packed. Edgar begged and borrowed the large sum (for those days) of three shillings and sixpence for a seat in the balcony, then gazed spellbound as Wilde – 'the ghost with a hammer in his hand' – bewildered his Aussie opponent with his brilliant foot and fist work.

Edgar considered Matty was out of form: 'he certainly looked the worse for wear after three rounds; he couldn't touch Wilde'.

Fund-raising

Almost as soon as they arrived the Australians were helping to raise money, not just for local charities but also for the war effort. On 8 March 1918 it was disclosed that £23,000 needed to be raised in Stroud district to purchase nine aeroplanes.

The Revd Hugh Towl of Bedford Street Congregational Church arranged with Wg/Cdr. Lt.-Col. Oswald Watt an 'air raid' on the town, dropping leaflets instead of bombs. Edgar Sollars remembers vividly the Australian air mechanics assembling an aeroplane on King Street Parade to the delight of the crowds that poured into the town.

Other towns in the area were also required to raise funds for aeroplanes which were, by early 1918, desperately required to compete against Germany's superior air force.

Mischief and Aerial Antics

Lt. Jack Butcher, one of the few non-Australian officers stationed at Leighterton, billeted on a nearby farm with his young wife Winifred, was responsible for the transport section at Leighterton. Jack told of escapades during his tour of duty there involving aerial deliveries:

> The Duke of Beaufort said he was short of sugar, so some bags were dropped on his front lawn. Then again there was a farmer who had a bull in a field which happened to be a short cut to the local pub. Some of these young Australians decided that they would have to do something about it. So, they dropped some sacks of potatoes and let them rattle over the farmhouse roof very early one morning. The bull was duly moved!

Jack remembered the Australians with great affection, perhaps because he had shared the horrors of Gallipoli with them in 1915. For the rest of his life he never mentioned what happened there, but often spoke of his time at Leighterton.

An Australian mechanic once goaded him into test-driving one of the huge motor vehicles, using the excuse that it had a fault which no one could trace. Jack dutifully drove it around the perimeter of the airfield. 'There's nothing wrong with it!' he exclaimed on his return.

'I know that,' said the Australian, 'It's just I didn't think a little bugger like you could drive it.'

In 1968, at the age of 75, Jack polished his medals and returned to Leighterton for the fiftieth Anniversary Anzac Day service. He was asked to stand on the dais and salute the march

Jack and Winifred Butcher at Leighterton, April 1918

past. 'It was one of the proudest days of his life,' said his daughter Pam.

Meanwhile the AFC pilots continued to attract attention. Their antics above the chimney-pots became notorious throughout the county, often being discussed at council meetings:

Councillor Aldridge drew attention to the practice of aviators flying low on Sundays over Stroud during service time and suggested that a letter be sent to the authorities asking for an alteration. Councillor Buscombe said a similar complaint had been made at Cirencester, with the result that aviators had to maintain an altitude of 2,000 feet.

Councillor Holloway said he had made a complaint about low flying at Amberley and the answer was that it was necessary to practise in this way. Whether it was necessary to do it on Sundays he could not say. Councillor Lambert associated himself with Councillor Aldridge in this matter and said he was glad to find him so anxious to secure the comfort of worshippers. (laughter.)

Stroud UDC minutes, July 1918

Some of the younger churchgoers, however, seemed quite happy to be disturbed in mid-sermon.

Canon Bob Kirby, born in 1907, was a choirboy at the time. He wrote this account for the Minchinhampton parish magazine some years ago and called it 'A Choirboy's Memories':

One of the excitements for us boys was the coming of the Australians to the Aerodrome at Aston. Some were billeted in the town and they joined in many of the social activities. We witnessed dare-devil stunts in canvas and wire machines, sometimes ending in disaster. I remember watching one pilot circling the church tower almost at clock level. Our heroes came to church, usually on Sunday evenings and we were able to see them at close and respectable quarters. Their chaplain, named Durnford, often preached – much better, we thought, than our own clergy. They also staged rodeos with buck jumping and stock whip cracking.

Canon Kirby himself moved to Australia, and lived and worked there for many years before his death in 1987.

Despite the interference with Sunday worship which dismayed councillors and churchmen, there were many who found the aerobatics of the AFC pilots highly entertaining. On weekdays, and indeed on Sundays, the road outside Minchinhampton Aerodrome swarmed with sightseers, anxious for a display. They were not usually disappointed, being treated to such tricks as the 'loop the loop', the 'falling leaf' which required great skill and courage, and the famous 'Immelman turn'.

One visitor to the 'drome' was 9-year-old Percy Hodges who, with his brother Arthur, aged 7, decided to walk from their home at Butterow to Minchinhampton to see the Aussie fliers. Not content with standing on the walls at Butterow, waving and cheering the planes as they flew over the Chalford valley, they felt it was worth the seven-mile trek to get closer to their heroes. They walked along the canal bank to Chalford, then up Cowcombe Hill to the new aerodrome which occupied both sides of the Minchinhampton–Cirencester road. In their haste they had forgotten to bring food or drink. They completed the journey, although Percy had to carry young Arthur 'piggy back' towards the end:

We sat on the stone wall and watched the aeroplanes going up and down like flies. We were near enough to see some of them starting the engines by swinging on their propellors. Sometimes they would wave out to us – I remember one red fighter, we called it 'the red devil'. (See Chapter 6.)

Percy also remembers seeing the Australians driving the big, solid-tyred lorries, calling at the dye works near his home to load boiler clinker to make up roads and paths at the aerodrome. 'We used to see them loading clinker every day of the week, including Sundays,' he recalled.

Two young sightseers just visible behind the wing of the aircraft at Minchinhampton, within touching distance of their heroes!

Activity at Minchinhampton, January 1919

'Ignition on – Contact!'

Despite attempts by the authorities to discourage people from attending the free air shows by such means as cancelling the buses, there were still many who made the journey to the aerodrome.

Chavenage

They used to drop in for coffee . . . landing on the lawn out-side the house.

Col. David Lowsley-Williams

Almost equidistant between Tetbury and Leighterton lie the house and grounds of Chavenage. This estate has a history going back to the time of the Civil War, and many relics of that period can be seen there. During the time the Australians were stationed nearby, it seems to have been 'open house' for them. Chavenage has been owned by the Lowsley-Williams family for several generations. And it was the grandparents of the present owner, Col. David Lowsley-Williams, who invited the Australians to dances, parties, and occasionally for morning coffee, sometimes with disastrous results.

In addition to the relics of the Civil War, the family have many souvenirs dating back to the 'Australian period' at Chavenage. As well as the aerial photographs (see Chapter 2), the family was presented with an album of more personal snapshots taken in the house and grounds.

In gratitude for the kind hospitality they experienced, the AFC officers also presented the family with a biscuit barrel carved from the propellor boss of a Sopwith Camel.

A disastrous visit to Chavenage. With aeroplanes costing up to £2,000 in 1918, this incident made for an expensive coffee break

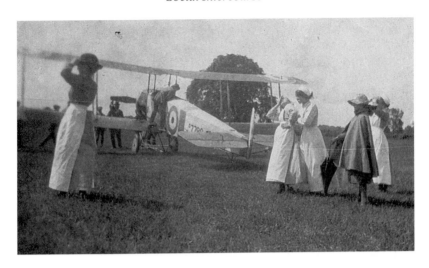

A day of circuits and bumps at Chavenage, summer 1918

A joyride in Kookaburra IV

David Lowsley-Williams with part of a propellor, the propellor boss and the presentation AFC photograph album

The Shows

They used to dress up as girls, using cottage loaves to give themselves a good bosom . . . that sort of thing.

Jack Sollars

No wartime entertainments could have been more popular than those put on by the AFC in Gloucestershire. These events were so well attended that extra late-night trains along the Chalford to Stonehouse line had to be laid on when they performed at the Stroud Subscription Rooms. In fact, they put on shows all over Gloucestershire. They performed regularly in Wotton-under-Edge, Tetbury, Dursley, Gloucester and Cirencester, as

Don't miss the
Event of the Year.

A.F.C. Concert Party

3rd Australian Entertainment

Gee=Whizz

SUBSCRIPTION ROOMS,
STROUD,
SATURDAY, NOVEMBER 30
at 7-30.

Prices 3/6 reserved, 2/6, 1/6

Bookings at Messrs Burr's Music Warehouse

Gee Whizz advertisement

well as appearing at smaller venues such as Amberley School (to raise money for a piano) and Minchinhampton Market Hall (to raise funds for the town's war memorial). Apart from the sheer fun they had in presenting these highly original shows, they were able to raise considerable sums of money for local hospitals, orphanages and wartime fund-raising schemes.

There were several different shows that toured the area. 'While the Billy Boils' was the first, and was so successful that it established a demand for more. The two bases ended up competing with each other for the best   The reviews. The Leighterton troupe called themselves 'The

---

IN AID OF LOCAL AND WAR CHARITIES,

THE A.F.C. CONCERT PARTY
(Minchinhampton Aerodrome) in their second Australian Night's Entertainment

"THE WELCOME NUGGET"
IN THE SUBSCRIPTION ROOMS, STROUD.

On Wednesday & Thursday, Aug. 28 & 29,
Commencing at 7-40 p m. sharp

This Entertainment, representing an Australian Goldmining Camp, with its special libretto, new music and scenic effects, should even eclipse the record success achieved by the A.F.C. Concert Party in "While the Billy Boils."

PRICES—(inclusive of Tax, and Souvenir Programme):
RESERVED SEATS 3/6
UNRESERVED SEATS ... ... 2/6 and 1/6

BOOKING,—Seats may be reserved, and tickets for the unreserved seats may be obtained in advance at Burr's Music House, George Street, Stroud, and at the Office of the Station Adjutant, Minchinahmpton Aerodrome. on and after Monday. the 26th inst.
REMEMBER that this Performance will not be repeated in Stroud and that many people were turned away last time, so SECURE SEATS EARLY.
LATE TRAINS.—By special arrangement with the G.W.R. the last Motor Train on both evenings will leave Chalford at 10 p,m. for all stations to Stonehouse ; and, on the return journey, will leave Stroud at 10.40 for all stations to Chalford.

Welcome Nugget advertisement

37

PUBLIC NOTICES

WOTTON-UNDER-EDGE

Grand Evening Concert

By the "FLYING KANGAROOS' from
Leighterton Aerodrome.
IN THE TOWN HALL
On SATURDAY, NOV. 2nd, at 8 p.m.
Programme to include the Sketch,
" Settled Up," in two acts.
Doors open 7.40. Ticket holders admitted
7.30.
Proceeds in aid of Funds of Wotton
Cricket Club and Extension of Y.M.C.A.
Hut, Leighterton.

In the Afternoon,
A FIRST-CLASS FOOTBALL MATCH
Australians (Leighterton) v. Army
Ordnance Corps (Gloucester)
will be played on the Grammar School
Field. Kick off 3 p.m. sharp. 3213

TOWN HALL,

SATURDAY'S CONCERT AT WOT-
TON-UNDER-EDGE. — "The Flying
Kangaroo" Concert Party from Leighterton Aerodrome gave the greatest delight
by their entertainment at Wotton Town
Hall on Saturday, each item of the well-
varied programme receiving well-merited
applause, and, in most cases, insistent demands for encores. The concert was arranged in aid of the local Cricket Club
funds, and also the extension of the
Y.M.C.A. Hut at Leighterton. Crowded
as the hall was, to its utmost capacity,
the financial result was most gratifying,
a profit of over £20 being made from
the concert and football match combined.
The local arrangements were undertaken
by Messrs. F. Holloway and J. Bassett,
with the able assistance of Messrs. F.
C. Ford and H. Jotcham, and C. A.
Pearce, and the Misses Bond and Shu-

Headlines and stories

tendance of clergy and prominent residents of the locality besides the widowed
mother, a brother and four sisters.
Bishop Mostyn performed the last rites.

FLYING KANGAROOS AT DURSLEY

SUCCESSFUL CONCERT BY AUSTRALIAN AIRMEN FROM LEIGHTERTON.

The Dursley Branch of the National
Federation of Discharged and Demobilised Sailors and Soldiers had a winner
on Wednesday evening in the Flying
Kangaroos (Australian Flying Corps
stationed at Leighterton, who
visited the town to give a concert on
behalf of the Branch funds. The concert
was in the large Men's Mess Room

SHORT NOTICE.

RETURN VISIT OF THE

Flying Kangaroos

(Australian Flying Corps Concert Party)

A NEW AND ENTIRE CHANGE OF
PROGRAMME.

To be held in THE MESS ROOM
(by kind permission of Messrs.
R. A. Lister and Co. Ltd.).

On TUESDAY, JANUARY 14, 1919
at 7.30 p.m.

POPULAR PRICES.

SECURE YOUR TICKETS EARLY.

Tickets may be obtained at the Gazette
Office, Castle Hotel, or any member of
the D.S. & S. Committee

Flying Kangaroos' and the entertainers from
Minchinhampton eventually settled for 'The Gee Whizzers'.

Even by today's standards these were lavish entertainments
utilizing not only performing skills, but expert scene-painting
and special effects. Vivid accounts in the local press give a
wonderful picture of the Aussies' fun-packed concerts. In particular they delighted in depicting scenes of their own homeland:

To convert the stage into an Australian gold mining camp
was no easy task, having regard to the limited space available for the purpose, but the illusion was cleverly achieved
by the brush of W. Merrick Boyd, the Australian artist, and
the smart acting and equipment of the dramatic company . . .
it says much for the ability of those responsible that the
brought the Southern Dominion right home to the audience.

The singing and acting throughout were delightful, and, as one might expect, were entirely free from vulgarity.

Stroud Journal, 'The Welcome Nugget', 31 August 1918

Among the individual performers, 2nd Air Mechanic Hulme was the resident comedian with the Flying Kangaroos:

Bob Hulme the humorist brought down the house with his monologue, 'The Military Representative', appearing in all the glory of a brass hat. He was equally successful in his absurdity, 'Who killed Bill Kaiser'.

Stroud Journal, 'Gee Whizz', 30 November 1918

Sgt Newson was, by all accounts, a great impressionist:

Flight Sergeant Newson's impersonation of a donkey was wonderfully plucky and clever.

Stroud Journal, 30 August 1918

Little is known of the off-stage lives of the performers, but Lt. Darcy Rees was a Flying Kangaroo in more ways than one. He seems to have led a chequered career as a pilot with 3rd Squadron AFC, before breaking nearly every bone in his body while trying to fly an aeroplane upside down at 50 ft! His good humour never left him though, and after the war he continued stunting around the civil aviation circuit in Australia. Whether or not he took part in any more shows is not recorded.

One of the most spectacular effects seen at Stroud Subscription Rooms was a replica of Minchinhampton aerodrome made for their last show, 'Coo-ee and Au Revoir':

The scene was rapidly changed to the Minchinhampton Aerodrome in the year 1918, an aeroplane occupying the foreground with the huge hangars behind. There was much tinkering with tools by mechanics in the work-a-day clothes, and the propellers being at last induced to turn at the call of 'contact' there was a sound of revolving machinery when alas the plane collapsed on the unfortunate officer in the pilot's seat. He was rescued amid hilarious laughter and on being asked if he was hurt replied, 'I do this every day.'

Stroud Journal

The aeroplane described was similar to one the Australians pulled through the streets of Stroud in the 'Monster Procession of Munitions Workers' on 31 August 1918.

Court Cases

High spirits, which sometimes got out of hand, meant the occasional appearance before local magistrates. Most cases involving men from the aerodromes were for minor infringements, such as riding bicycles without lamps. Some were rather more serious.

Stroud magistrates recommended that three men from Minchinhampton 'drome' were sent 'back to the front, forthwith' for stealing a pair of boots worth 3s. 6d. from Taylors shoe shop in Stroud.

In the Dursley Court, which served Leighterton aerodrome, the magistrates appear to have been equally severe. A local 16-year-old who stole a clock received four years in Borstal. Two young boys were each given six strokes of the birch for the crime of stealing three eggs (and a custodial sentence was

The 'Monster Procession' through Stroud on 31 August 1918, organized by the munitions factory workers: the AFC model aeroplane

Part of the fancy dress parade

The munitions factory workers

A local float with an aeronautical theme

promised for any repetition). When a colonial found himself up before the bench, his thoughts might well have travelled back a mere fifty years to a time when transportation to Australia was a common punishment meted out to his ancestors who faced similar courts.

Any offence connected with the theft of animals provoked ferocious sentencing from magistrates in farming districts. On 12 April 1919, a few weeks before they were due to go home, at a special sitting of Tetbury magistrates, two Australian air mechanics and a civilian were charged with stealing a pig.

At the trial, no fewer than four policemen from three different police stations, five witnesses, the three defendants, and the corpse of the pig itself appeared before the bench.

The dead pig was one of five belonging to Capt. John Doe of the RAF, and was kept behind the canteen at Leighterton aerodrome. On the morning of 9 April, Harold Peer of Nailsworth, employed by Captain Doe's wife to care for the pigs, was dismayed to find there were only four left. Furthermore he saw bloody evidence that the missing pig had been assassinated (but apparently not gutted) in its own sty. In the soft earth between the piggeries he found tracks left by a pony and trap.

The following afternoon, Mr and Mrs Mathews who ran a grocery-cum-bakery-cum-tea shop in Church Street, Wotton-under-Edge, were offered, and purchased, a saddle-back pig. It was carried into the shop by two Australians in uniform. Mr Mathews said in Court that, although both of the accused soldiers had previously lodged at his house, he could not swear they were the two Australians who manhandled the pig on to his shop scales for weighing.

On 11 April, PS Baker (Wotton) and PC Sheppard (Charfield) visited Arthur Dickinson at home in Tresham in order to examine the hooves and wheels of his pony and trap. PC Forty (Kingscote) had earlier phoned through a description of the prints found at the piggery. The officers concluded that they were identical to Arthur's conveyance and promptly took him to Tetbury Police Station where he made the following statement:

I was at Leighterton Aerodrome on Tuesday night. I was asked to take a pig to Wotton to sell it and they told me it was their own pig. They killed it in the sty and asked me to sell it at Wotton. I took it to Mrs Mathews and sold it. They (Ted Williams and a man called 'Joe the Butcher') came down with me to Wotton. They received the money (£7 9s.) and I received 10s. back. The pig was not burned or dressed.

Ted Williams and 'Joe the Butcher' turned out to be Robert Henry Williams and Thomas Henry Mitchell, both of the AFC and both due to board the boat for home on 6 May. They could remember little of the night in question, it having been one of those rare evenings when strong liquor had been flowing at the canteen. They were more than willing to accept 'Transportation for life' as punishment.

After three hours of listening to the evidence, and in view of the seriousness of the charge, the magistrates had no alternative but to commit the accused for trial at the next Gloucester Assizes to be held on 12 June 1919, five weeks after the boat was to have taken the Australians home. They were remanded in custody and Arthur was allowed bail of £50.

Having literally 'missed the boat', the two Australians pleaded for leniency from Mr Justice Bray at Gloucester Assizes. The judge reckoned Mitchell ('Joe the Butcher') and Williams were guilty of killing the pig at the sty and opening it at Arthur's house, the offal having been buried in his back garden. Arthur was convicted of receiving a stolen pig. All three received three-month prison sentences. This was reduced to two months for the Australians, as they had been in custody since 12 April.

The Armistice Celebrations

An armistice was officially declared on 11 November 1918. The desire to celebrate, particularly of the young, brought calls for restraint from those in authority. The Australians, however, could not wait to let off steam.

PREMATURE ARMISTICE CELEBRATION IN STROUD

Wild scenes were occasioned in Stroud and at a local aerodrome on Thursday night last week by the premature announcement regarding the signing of the Armistice. The newspaper statements concerning the matter were not sufficient to disturb the customary equilibrium of residents generally, but at about ten o'clock the town was invaded by a couple of hundred Australian soldiers, who, with their band kept up a lively din until the 'wee sma' hours' of Friday morning. They played and sang and a number of the fair sex joined in the jubilations, but the townsfolk as a whole were too dubious to lend countenance to the celebration. The return of the Australian soldiers to their camp was the occasion for a further display of hilarity.

Stroud Journal

On the night itself, airmen in Tetbury decided to set the town alight. It is said they took a bowser (a large container of

NAILSWORTH POLICE COURT.

THURSDAY.—Before Col. H. G. Ricardo (in the chair), Messrs. S. J. Newman, M. H. Grist, J. T. Ramsay and A. C. Blake.

Obscene Language.

William James Risby, a labourer, of Avening, was fined 5s. for having made use of obscene language at Nailsworth on April 5th.

No Lights.

Kenneth James Knowlton, of the Australian Flying Corps, summoned for riding a bicycle without a light at Minchinhampton, was, on the evidence of Special Constable Excell, fined 5s.

Dismissed.

Norman Hall, of the Australian Flying Corps, was summoned for driving a motor car to the danger of the public at Box, Minchinhampton, on March 8th.

P.C. Dance stated that when defendant was driving at the Box he ran into a cart belonging to Mr. Viney, which was standing at the side of the road, and did damage to the extent of £7.

Defendant was defended by Mr. A. L. Lane, and the case was dismissed.

Nailsworth police court column, Stroud Journal

The Leighterton flag cartoon

petrol) into Long Street at midnight and emptied the contents down the length of it. The resulting conflagration was short-lived, but spectacular.

Australians celebrating at the Falcon Inn in Tetbury drew a cartoon on a flag to commemorate the occasion. They called it the Leighterton flag and it hangs today in the RAAF Museum at Point Cook, Victoria.

Marriages

Love affairs between local girls and Australians were often discouraged. The 12,000 miles to the other side of the world that a young bride might be taken must have seemed an incredible distance to concerned parents.

Among the marriages that did occur was a unique double wedding involving two AFC men and sisters Eunice and Miriam Bassett from Ebley.

Miriam married Sgt Nick Reyne AFC. He stayed on in the Stroud area after the war and started up the Red Bus Company, operating out of the Austral Garage in Lansdown. The kangaroo emblem on the buses is still remembered in the district.

Those couples wishing to settle in Australia had to wait a little longer for a different boat. Among these were William Stuart Nash and his new bride Doris Brews from 'Glenroy', Minchinhampton. Doris was the daughter of golfing professional George Brews.

From Marryatville in South Australia their daughter Jose writes:

My parents met at a musical function in Minchinhampton put on for the benefit of the men at Leighterton. I believe my mother sang 'Roses of Picardy' when Dad first clapped eyes on her. Evidently the local Rector organized hot baths for the soldiers and he used to interrupt the proceedings and point to a soldier and say, 'Friend, your bath is ready.' At this stage Dad had been away [from Australia] for five years and was due to come home on leave. Evidently the ship got out into the channel and armistice was declared so it came back again and they all had more leave. So my parents decided to get married and they came out together by ship.

A DOUBLE WEDDING AT EBLEY.

England and Australia.

A great deal of interest was manifested in a double wedding that took place on Thursday in the Ebley Congregational Chapel, when the nuptials were solemnised of two English maidens and two Australian soldiers. The brides were Misses Eunice and Miriam Bassett, third and fourth daughters of Mr. and Mrs. Ira J. Bassett, of Springville, Ebley, and their stalwart bridegrooms were A/M Montague Rawlins Garbutt, A.F.C., son of Mr. W. A. Garbutt, of, Newcastle, Australia, and Sergt. Nicholas Derrick Reyne, A.F.C., son of Mr. Dirk Reyne, of Melbourne. The bridesmaids were the Misses Amy and Ruth Bassett, and the bestmen were A.M. J. A. Casey and Flight-Sergt. J. Stratton, also of the A.F.C. It was a pretty sight in the Church to see the youthful brides enter one on either arm of their father. They looked charming in dresses of ivory satin and jewel net and wreaths and veils, and like the bridesmaids carried beautiful bouquets. Misses Amy and Ruth Bassett wore dresses of mauve cashmere and georgette with black and mauve hats. Mr. Bassett, father of the brides, gave them away, and the ceremony was performed by Rev. J. Burton, assisted by the Rev. R. Nott. By the courtesy of Mr. John Jacob, Mr. A. M. Boucher, who numbers the brides among his music pupils, played wedding music. A reception was held at Springville, after much snapshotting of the party, and in the evening Mr. and Mrs. Garbutt left for Penzance, and Mr. and Mrs. Reyne motored to Cheltenham for the respective honeymoons. Both bridal couples will return to Stroud for a few months until they eventually leave for Australia. Eunice wore a travelling dress of mauve and Miriam a blue silk dress, and both wore powder blue coats with hats to match. The bridegroom's present to Eunice was a propellor clock and pair of tips, and Miriam received a wristlet watch from her bridegroom; and presented him with a signet ring. The presents to both brides from the parents were cheques.

Wedding report, Stroud Journal

Reyne wedding certificate

Doris Elsie Brews, 1918

Nash wedding certificate

William Nash and Doris Brews, Minchinhampton, 1918

Alfred and Alice Taylor on their wedding day in Tetbury, June 1920

And how my mother put up with being so far from her home and family in those days I cannot imagine especially as there were no jet planes to get back quickly. I have the greatest admiration for her. She took my brother and me back in 1923 for six months and she didn't go back again until I took her in 1976 when she was 80 years of age.

Among those who stayed in the district after getting married were Alfred and Alice Taylor, the parents of David Taylor who still lives in Tetbury. Before the war his father had been an engineer living south of Geelong in Victoria. Alfred enlisted in April 1915 and saw action in Gallipoli and France. During the freezing winter of 1917 he was stationed in Bapaume, where he heard that volunteers were required to join the AFC. He felt life would be better in the air force and clear of the trenches.

1st Wing AFC HQ Transport, Tetbury. Alfred Taylor is in the back row, furthest left

When the AFC Wing was set up at Tetbury Father was a 1st Class Air Mechanic attached to the Transport section. His duty was to go on twice weekly runs to Bristol to bring the food supplies for Tetbury, Leighterton and Minchinhampton. I think they used to run three lorries twice a week. . . . Mother was a Tetbury girl, her family had been in Tetbury for many generations. Her father had been a baker, surname Hill. Father had to go back to Australia to be demobilized and he wanted my mother to go as well. Her mother maintained a strong control on her and said, 'I won't let you go.' My (Tetbury) grandmother claimed my mother would get out to Australia only to find that the man she'd gone to marry was already married or would desert her. She said to my father, 'If you want to marry Alice you'll have to come to Tetbury.' So that was that – he went to Australia to be demobbed and spent a few months looking around his family and came back in February 1920 and they got married in the June. He stayed in Tetbury the rest of his life and didn't go back to Australia.

David Taylor

*David Taylor at home in Tetbury
with his collection of AFC
memorabilia*

CHAPTER 4

Three Australian Personalities

Lt.-Col. Oswald Watt OBE, CO of the 1st wing

I am an Australian and I don't have any manners.
Oswald Watt

It was said of Col. 'Toby' Watt that he was 'an Australian to his fingertips'. In fact he was educated in England at Clifton College and Cambridge. While commanding the training wing from his HQ in Tetbury, he forged many friendships and earned the lifelong respect of the men under him.

He came to Tetbury in March 1918 at the age of 40 with a remarkable service record behind him. He had joined the French Foreign Legion (Aviation Militaire section) at the outbreak of war, and before Britain had made up its mind to join in. By the time he left in January 1916, he had been decorated with the Legion of Honour and the Croix de Guerre (with Palms) by General ('Papa') Joffre on the field.

Watt spent a brief time in Egypt with 1st Squadron AFC before taking command of 2nd Squadron AFC, which he trained in England and took to France early in 1917:

Major Watt trained his squadron to such a pitch of excellence that I have no hesitation in saying that it was one of

Lt.-Col. Oswald Watt AFC, OBE,
Legion of Honour, Croix de Guerre

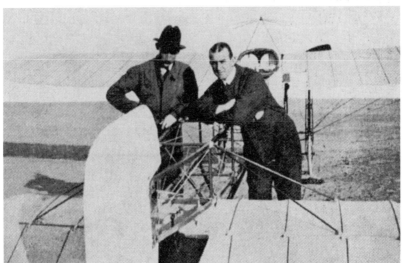

Oswald Watt in his Bleriot monoplane 'Malleleu', Egypt 1913/14

the best Squadrons that has left England for service with the Expeditionary Force.

J.M. Salmond (Maj.-Gen. Commanding
Training Division, Royal Flying Corps).

While leading his squadron from England across the channel to Warloy in France, Watt removed his goggles and inserted his monocle to consult a map, whereupon his machine went into a half roll, spilling map and monocle into the sea. Unable to navigate he assumed position at the rear of the squadron and was led to base by one of the other pilots.

Despite the excellent reputation of 2nd Squadron, his style of leadership did not always meet with British approval. The tale is told of 'Mac', a young pilot, who performed the 'zoom' take-off despite repeated orders to the contrary. Eventually 'Mac' stalled the engine of his DH5 on take-off and narrowly averted a serious crash:

'Awfully sorry, Sir, I really won't do it again.'

'No, please don't,' said Watt, and after a short homily, 'and now go to your room, sit on the end of your bed and for a quarter of an hour say to yourself, "what a bloody fool I was".'

In November 1917 during General Byng's attack on Cambrai, eighteen Sopwith Camels flying low in thick fog attacked the enemy on the ground with bombs and machine-guns. Six of the pilots were awarded the Military Cross for their part in the raid; the other twelve were killed.

Tetbury turned out to be the headquarters of the biggest command ever held by an Australian aviator in wartime.

Watt's technical knowledge, together with his concern for the welfare of the trainees, made Leighterton and Minchinhampton the envy of other flying schools of the time. Cadet pilots were encouraged to work alongside their mechanics

The six sole survivors of no. 2 squadron AFC who came to Minchinhampton and Leighterton as instructors. Left to right: Capt. L. Holden MC, AFC, Maj. R.C. Phillips MC, DFC, AFC, Capt. W.A. Robertson, Lt. H. Clark, Oswald Watt, Lt. R.L. Clark

and the mechanics in turn were made to take test rides in the machines they had serviced, the tragic aspect of this being that they featured in some of the accidents.

Many innovations were made in the industrious atmosphere of the workshops including the engine Escarget, portable rocking machines, and the appearing and disappearing aeroplanes for gunnery practice set up at Long Newton.

In January 1919, Watt was awarded an OBE. There were some who felt his outspokenness had 'ruffled a few feathers' and held up greater honours.

Inside the Minchinhampton engine workshop

The engine repair section at Leighterton 1918, still standing (1992) but used as a potato store

Gunnery practice at Long Newton

When he got home in July 1919 Watt headed for his beloved camp at Bilgola, a few miles north of Sydney. Bilgola was part of an old rain forest that had survived because of its remoteness and the shelter provided by the surrounding hills. It comprised seven acres of near tropical scenery with an abundance of cabbage-tree palms, burrawongs, wattles and eucalyptus gums. It gave a glorious view of the Pacific Ocean. It was also one of the most dangerous coves on the eastern seaboard of Australia.

During the next two years he ran a private repatriation unit from his office in Sydney, to give his 'boys' a fair start in civilian life. As President of the Australian Aero Club he inaugurated a 'Safety First' campaign. This resulted in several Acts

Bilgola, NSW

Watt's house, Bilgola

of Parliament designed to achieve better safety standards in civil aviation throughout Australia.

Gathering firewood early on the morning of 21 May 1921, Watt slipped on the rocks at Bilgola, struck his head, and as the tide came in he drowned in a few inches of water. He was found floating out to sea by his manservant Jones, several hours later.

His ashes were interred at St Jude's church, Randwick, NSW. Bearers at his funeral included men who had served with him in France, Leighterton and Minchinhampton.

In the family vault were placed the AFC pennant, his airman's helmet and his goggles.

Watts funeral cortège, Randwick, NSW

Walter Oswald Watt. 'He was a great man and a great soldier.' (Gen. Jobson, 23 May 1921)

Ernest Howard Jefferys

Ernest Jefferys arrived at Minchinhampton in July 1918 to learn the art of aerial combat. He was aged 23 and known to his friends as 'Jeffy'.

Like most of the ANZACs at Leighterton and Minchinhampton, Ernest had seen action in Gallipoli and France before being accepted as a cadet pilot. His war record is typical of many of the young cadets.

On 17 October 1914, Ernest sailed on HMS *Suffolk* with the 2nd Battalion, 1st Brigade AIF, and was among the first to wade ashore at Gallipoli on 25 April 1915 (Anzac Day). He was injured twice during his time at Gallipoli, the second time receiving a head wound which was serious enough to merit hospitalization in England.

In November 1916, Ernest was posted to the Western Front and saw action in Flanders, Fricourt, Hermies, Triancourt, Mametz Wood, Bapaume, Beaumetz Wood and Bullecourt. On 4 May 1917 he received a gunshot wound to the left shoulder. The rest of 1917 was spent in England where he qualified as a wireless operator on 18 January 1918. During this time he met up with an old childhood sweetheart, Gertie Dowsett, who had volunteered as a VAD nurse and now found herself in England with Ernest and some free time.

An oversight for which he was not responsible meant that Ernest accidentally went AWOL for a couple of days in September 1917. For this he was demoted from Sergeant to Corporal and lost eleven days' pay.

When the newly formed AFC advertised for recruits, Ernest applied and was accepted. His preliminary training complete, he travelled from Uxbridge to Tetbury on 25 July to begin

E.H. Jefferys before leaving Australia for Gallipoli in 1914

practical training in aerial combat. He was detailed to the 6th Training Squadron at Minchinhampton.

On 28 August 1918 at 7.00 a.m. he was sent up for a practice flight. By 7.25 a.m. he was dead.

Kuring-Gai railway station, 1914, run by Ernest's father. Ernest is on the right

Ernest recovering from his wounds in hospital at Devonport, 1917

Gertie, harbour master, Ernest and dog, at Mevagissey, Cornwall, in June 1917

Gertie and Ernest, Devon, June 1917

Devon, June 1917

Ernest at Beaconsfield, early 1918

Ernest on leave in Oxford, May 1918

July 1918, the last picture of E.H. Jefferys

A triple funeral at Leighterton, 31 August 1918. Gertie is supported by two of Ernest's mates.

Harry Cobby DSO, DFC and Bars

Harry Cobby was one of the most famous of the 'aces' of the First World War. He destroyed twenty-nine enemy aeroplanes during his time with 4th squadron AFC, which made him the highest-scoring Australian pilot. He came to Leighterton as an aerial combat instructor in 1918. He considered this job more dangerous than dog-fighting itself. On arrival at Leighterton he chose the best Camel available and had it painted black and white in a chequerboard style.

Fearless in the air, on the ground he was a fun-loving character. He enjoyed taking part in the hunt at nearby Badminton, with little regard for the niceties of the English class system. Cobby's evenings were spent visiting Bristol, Bath, Cheltenham and Gloucester, but it was the Kings Head Hotel in Cirencester that he enjoyed most. The proprietor, Mr Brockman, seems to have made all the Australians especially welcome.

On returning to Australia Cobby became a founder member of the RAAF, which was formed in 1921. During the Second World War he was Commander of the First Tactical Air Force at Noemoor and Morotai Islands. He died on 11 November 1952.

Capt. H. Cobby DSO, DFC and bars, in his chessboard Camel, 1918

An AFC dinner at the King's Head Hotel, Cirencester

CHAPTER 5

Crashes and Casualties

Fatalities

The question asked by most visitors to Leighterton cemetery is: 'Why did these young Australians die in training?' The truth is that many early cadet pilots lost their lives while learning the new skills required by the latest aeroplanes. One of the many tragic statistics is that seven out of the twenty-five graves have dates *after* the Armistice. From an Australian military point of view it was important to continue to develop the AFC for the future defence of its own shores. So training in aerial offence and defence continued after the war.

Of the twenty-five buried at Leighterton, one man died of heart failure in a local pub, one from appendicitis, three from Spanish flu, which was at epidemic proportions in the winter of 1918, and one as a result of a road accident at Barton End; but the great majority, seventeen men, died in crashing aircraft. There were at least another seven deaths but these men were buried elsewhere.

The single-seater fighter, the Sopwith Camel, was the most efficient warplane at the time. It had been brought into full production in the middle of 1917 and took great skill to fly properly. Although this aeroplane was not involved in all the accidents at Leighterton and Minchinhampton, it was high on the list of crashed machines. It had a rotary engine, which meant that a large part of the engine mass spun round with the propellor, making directional control of the aeroplane difficult. It had only been in the middle of the war that an RFC Officer, Maj. Smith-Barry, had mastered the art of recovering from a diving spin, which hitherto had been 100 per cent fatal. So, although the theory of spin recovery was well known by the time the AFC started training in the Cotswolds, it still needed to be taught in real aeroplanes to inexperienced pilots, along with all the other dangerous manoeuvres necessary for survival in war.

Perfectly preserved specimens of all the types of aircraft in use at the two airfields – the Sopwith Camel, the Avro 504K, the Bristol Fighter, the SE5, and many more – are on exhibition at the RAF museum at Hendon. Seeing these machines at close quarters highlights the conditions under which First World War pilots operated, their lives literally depending on threads of wire and sheets of canvas holding together under very great stress.

The accident with the largest death toll happened on 28 August 1918, on the very day the AFC were preparing to put on their stage show at the Stroud Subscription Rooms. Ironically, 'The Golden Nugget' was a show that contained a comedy sketch based on an air crash.

At about 7.20 a.m. on that day, a single-seater Avro DH6 flown by Lt. Ernest Jefferys, and a twin-seater Avro 504 containing Lt. Charles Scott and Lt. Roy Cummings, were both at around 1,500 ft near Minchinhampton aerodrome. Evidence given at the inquest by Sgt. Henry Griffiths indicated that one machine was doing a climbing left turn in an easterly direction and the other was flying in a westerly direction. The climbing machine struck the other underneath, probably because the visibility of the climbing aircraft was cut off. Both machines immediately fell to earth. Although not documented, this

Graves at Leighterton

appears to be an instance of 'sham' fighting which ended in disaster for both pursuer and quarry.

Just ten days previously on 18 August, two experienced pilots, Lt. Harry Taylor and Lt. Douglas Ferguson from Minchinhampton, were carrying out dogfighting manoeuvres over the church at Shipton Moyne. While divine service was in progress they collided in mid-air, and both died in the resulting fall to the ground. Lt. Taylor was buried in Birmingham and Lt. Ferguson in Cirencester, where he had friends.

The last AFC airman to lose his life in the Cotswolds was Cadet Thomas Keen MC, on 12 March 1919. He was under instruction from Capt. Les Holden, both fliers having left Rendcomb aerodrome at 9.55 a.m. in single-seater aeroplanes. They were manoeuvring around Cirencester and Miserden Park when Cadet Keen flew into fog. Unable to find his pupil, Les Holden returned to Minchinhampton. Cadet Keen had collided with a tree in Miserden Park. A land girl named Excell was working about 100 yards away from the crash site and ran to help the aviator. There was nothing she could do to save him.

Lucky Escapes

Not all the aeroplane accidents were fatal.

During the Armistice month of November 1918, Maj. Phillips of 6th Squadron was happy to report no fatal accidents, just one or two near misses:

Whilst on formation flying in an SE5, the engine of Lieut. Syme's machine cut out at 1000 ft. There being no large fields

This is Avro 504 D7785 which managed to straddle a Cotswold stone wall, while attempting to land near Leighterton. Happily both occupants survived. Jack Butcher took the photograph, and his wife Winifred can be seen with their pet dog on the extreme right of the picture

within gliding distance he attempted to land in a small area. The inevitable happened. The machine ran across the field and crashed into a stone wall. The pilot was uninjured but the machine was a 'write-off'. Lt. C.L. Vaileu had a unique experience. Whilst diving at the ground target the propeller of his machine, an SE5, flew off. The engine 'overrevved' and the radiator burst. By skilful manoeuvre the pilot managed to land the machine safely in a field near the aerodrome.

Squadron Commander's Report extract, November 1918

Another crash, unfortunately not photographed, happened at Painswick on 12 April 1918. The newspaper story is headed 'Serious accident at Painswick' and subtitled 'Children charged and injured by an aeroplane'. Had the Australian pilot taken leave of his senses? Were Cotswold children being used to practise trench strafing? Or was it merely bad proof-reading at the *Stroud Journal*?

None of these alternatives hint at the truth, which in many ways is even more bizarre than fiction.

Lt. H. Fisher-Webster was on a training flight from Minchinhampton aerodrome on the morning of 12 April when he ran out of fuel and was obliged to descend rather quickly. He was fortunate enough to land unhurt in a field near Hill Farm, Holcombe, Painswick, run by a Mr J.H. Westcott. The aeroplane was quite undamaged by the experience.

Pte. Jones, who happened to be passing at the time, saw the landing and on instructions from Fisher-Webster made off for Minchinhampton aerodrome to advise the authorities.

While Fisher-Webster waited for assistance by his machine, a large crowd of schoolchildren had gathered to watch the fun, lining the perimeter of the field.

Help eventually arrived in the form of a party from the aerodrome bearing fuel and a replacement pilot, Lt. W. Stanley Martin. He was to fly the aeroplane back to base in place of the unfortunate Fisher-Webster. To do this it was decided to move the machine to a more favourable take-off position at the top of the field. Mr Westcott offered the services of his steam tractor to tow the plane up the incline. The AFC gratefully accepted the offer. Being a wettish April, the ground was fairly soft and the tractor left deep ruts in the field as it puffed up the hill.

The aeroplane was started up and Lt. Martin, cheered on by the crowd, revved up and started back down the field. It was then that the plane was drawn inexorably towards the ruts made by the steam tractor. The left wheel dropped into the gully and the machine careered out of control towards the hurriedly dispersing crowd of onlookers. The aeroplane now had a mind of its own and pursued them through a fence into the next field. By the time it came to rest the machine was a write-off and the field was strewn with injured schoolchildren. Among the casualties were Frederick Reeks of Lyncombe Farm with a fractured right leg, William Parsons of the Park, Isobel Swayne of Vicarage Street, Ivy Brown of Paradise and Violet Allen Hambutts, all bruised and cut and in a state of shock.

The casualties were conveyed to Stroud Hospital in an AFC motor lorry, and everyone except the boy Reeks was sent home in bandages.

Obviously this was a serious incident at the time, but there were no fatalities and all involved made a good recovery. Frederick Reeks was probably able to dine out for many years afterwards with the tale of how he got a broken leg in a plane crash during the First World War!

Another crash in the summer of 1918 was photographed by Bill Nash. The location is not recorded, but it provides a fascinating insight into the method of crash recovery.

A Sopwith Camel at the end of its final approach to a forced landing. The presence of a number of civilians including a small child and no ambulance suggests that the pilot emerged unscathed. A caped policeman stands at a safe distance and an AFC mechanic is ready with a petrol can to siphon off fuel

The Camel, now without wings, wheels and engine cowling, is guyed with ropes to pull it the right way up. A small child observes from dangerously close quarters

The wreck is now safely stowed on a trailer, towed by a Rolls Royce recovery wagon

The ill-fated machine is towed through a local town, surrounded by interested bystanders and an inquisitive horse

A number of other crash photographs have come to light, none unfortunately with the time and place identified, but all bearing either the kangaroo or emu insignia which indicated the Leighterton and Minchinhampton bases, respectively. The boomerang seen on some of the photographs was in use with 4th Squadron AFC in France. Some of those machines also appeared (and crashed) in the district.

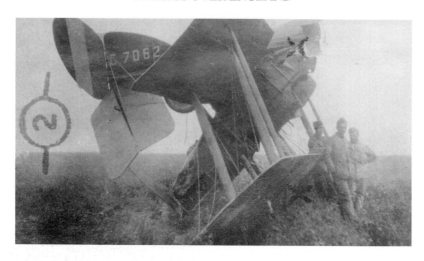

CHAPTER 6

Myths and Legends

The Red Baron

*There was one aircraft we saw often which we were told was
the captured Fokker belonging to the infamous 'Red Baron'
Richthofen.*

Jack Sollars

There were many strange and new sights to be seen in the air
over Stroud district in 1918/19, but not the Red Baron's aircraft. Manfred von Richthofen was shot down on 21 April
1918. The wreck of the famous Red Fokker DR1 Triplane,
which he was flying at the time, was picked over by souvenir
hunters and little of it remained by the time RAF investigators
arrived at the scene. Instructor Capt. Les Holden did, however,
have an SE5 which he had painted bright red and which put in
many flying hours over the Cotswolds.

All the instructors had their machines personalized. There
were coloured dragon emblems, aircraft painted all black for
night-flying, kookaburra, emu and kangaroo insignia, and even
rainbow-coloured aeroplanes. Capt. Cobby had a chequerboard
Camel, Capt. Garnie Malley's was pure white, and Capt.
'Tabby' Pflaum sported a 'joey' mascot on the fuselage of his
SE5. This latter instructor was, by all accounts, a bit of a

Capt. Les Holden, pilot of the red SE5

prankster and often played practical jokes. On one occasion he 'buzzed' the billet of Lt.-Col. Watt in Tetbury very early one morning. Although unable to identify the culprit on that occasion, Watt insisted that Pflaum's nickname should be marked on the side of his machine so that he could be clearly identified thereafter.

A more pressing reason for the distinguishable colours was the need for visibility during 'sham' dogfighting. The dangerous manoeuvres involved in this put instructors and cadets at extreme risk. Some instructors found that three or four mock fights per day were as stressful as flying in France.

Clearly, the more visible an instructor was to his pupil, the better.

An all white Avro 504 with the Flying Kangaroo emblem

A Leighterton Avro 504 decorated with a dragon

89

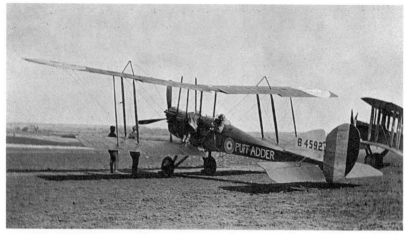

'Puff Adder' about to take off from Leighterton

German Sabotage

Stories circulated that perhaps some of the AFC fatalities were caused by German spies sabotaging aircraft. From documented facts on the crashes there seems little evidence of this. Following each fatal accident the local coroner (Mr Morton-Ball at Minchinhampton) called in the AFC ground crew at crash inquests to testify that the machines were in sound condition before taking off. There were indeed German prisoners of war at Leighterton who may have fuelled the conjecture about spies. However, judging by the appearance of these dejected prisoners, they were incapable of sabotage work.

The German POWs at Leighterton are believed to have been employed pumping water to the base from a nearby well. Three who managed to escape were quickly recaptured.

German POWs

Cornfields into Airfields

Local farmers started feeling the draught once the airfields got into service, resulting in a little myth-making. At a Chipping Sodbury Farmers' Union meeting in April 1918, it was maintained that great numbers of workers were being enticed away from the land by the high wages offered at the airfields, thus seriously curtailing food production. They urged the authorities to rethink their policies before the population starved to death. Yet, though stringent rationing was in force during 1918 and 1919, there is no record of mass malnutrition locally, despite the continued presence of the airfields. A worker who had 'done his bit' at Leighterton Aerodrome was moved to pick up his pen and reply to the farmers' complaint:

LEIGHTERTON

THE LABOUR QUESTION. – A correspondent who signs himself as 'One who has done his bit', writes with reference to the action of the Chipping Sodbury Branch of the Gloucestershire Farmers' Union in protesting against the Aeroplane Company in the neighbourhood enticing men off the land by offering them high wages. He contends that the average wage which is being paid by farmers to their labourers to-day is quite inadequate to meet the high cost of living, and says that if they won't pay a living wage the men have a perfect right in this free country to go where they can secure better remuneration. The policy of the farmers on this matter, he adds, is like that of the dog in the manger: they won't pay their men a living wage and then make a stir when they go elsewhere to get it.

The 'Leighterton Resolution' tabled by Wotton-under-Edge parish council reflects the strength of feeling among local employers:

HIGH WAGES AT LEIGHTERTON

Wotton-under-Edge Parish Council have sent copies of the appended resolutions to the Ministry of Munitions, Board of Agriculture, Dursley District Council, Sir Charles Bathurst, MP, Mr Ben Bathurst, MP, and Mr Athelstan Rendall, MP:

'That this meeting strongly deprecates the high rate of wages paid to the casual labourers at the Leighterton Aerodrome, especially having regard to the ages and physical conditions of many of them, and which is to the detriment of local industries, particularly of food production.'

An unusually frank letter in the *Dursley Gazette* from 'A casual labourer' puts the case for the workers. He contended that Leighterton was the worst paid airfield in England:

HIGH WAGES AT LEIGHTERTON

To the Editor of the Gazette.

Sir – I was very much surprised to read the Wotton-under-Edge Parish Council's resolution re the above. Will the Wotton Parish Council kindly give the names of the casual labourers who by their presence at Leighterton are a detriment to food production: Is this food production; camouflage?

It is a great pity the Wotton Parish Council has nothing better to occupy their time than to find fault with high wages, as Leighterton aerodrome is one of the worst paid in England. We are expecting a rise on Friday next, and it will be thankfully received by

ONE OF THE CASUAL LABOURERS

This was followed by a letter from Lancashire, warning the authors of the Leighterton Resolution to remember the power of the ballot box at the forthcoming general election, a foretaste of the growing militancy of workers:

WAGES AT LEIGHTERTON

To the Editor of the Gazette

Sir – being a native of Wotton-under-Edge, and a regular reader of the Gazette I was astonished at the resolution passed (re high wages at the aerodrome at Leighterton) by the Wotton-under-Edge Parish Council. I thought their duty was to report progress and look to the interests of the people who put them there. Workers, remember this next polling time, and take the lesson to heart. Now is the time for you to assert yourselves. Intimidation is dead. See that you give it a headstone called Justice. The chance to get a better existence down there is like a drop from the ocean compared with Lancashire, yet no Council dare such resolutions here as the masters are taught to respect a worker for what he is worth by the various unions.

Feeling isolated by the recipients of their controversial resolution and roundly condemned by the workers, Wotton parish council went no further with their foray into industrial relations.

Unanimous Hero Worship

It cannot be denied that the overwhelming majority of the population treated the Aussies like latter-day pop idols. There were pockets of indifference, however, verging sometimes on belligerence, especially at the town hall in Tetbury where things got very testy quite early on.

In April 1918 the town clerk was already pleading with the Road Board in Whitehall to provide 300 tons of stone urgently required for road maintenance 'due to the extraordinary traffic in connection with the new aerodrome at Leighterton'.

On 8 April the clerk requested £3 from the AFC 'for the repair to the Long Street bracket lamp damaged by lorry number 996390'. At the April council meeting it was decided to accept £2 15s. from the driver, Mr A. Taylor (David Taylor's Australian-born father) in settlement 'if the sum is paid at once'. With the evidence against them and the 5s. discount, Wing HQ paid up.

Troubles mounted for the harassed town clerk. He wrote to the Petrol Control Committee in London on 18 April, requesting a larger petrol ration: 'There is a considerable number of Military billeted in the town which is the Wing HQ of Leighterton and Minchinhampton. Naturally there is an increased demand for water for domestic purposes ...' It appears that extra water had to be transported into the town by tanker, hence the request for a larger petrol allowance, which of course was rationed.

On 9 May in a further letter to Lt.-Col. Watt at Wing HQ, the clerk revealed that another lamp post had been damaged in Long Street near Lloyds Bank: 'broken by a motor lorry, damage estimated at £3 10s. The driver of the lorry cleared off and I have been unable to ascertain the number . . .'.

There followed a one-sided correspondence to the AFC who, realizing there was no incriminating evidence this time, decided to ignore requests for payment. By 10 October 1918, the bill, inflated to £4 12s. 6d., had not even been formally acknowledged. On 23 March 1919 the AFC grudgingly replied to the *fifth* request for payment, but asked for proof of liability. The town clerk testily pointed out in his reply: '. . . no doubt if the enquiry had been made by your men when I first wrote to you last year, the driver could have been ascertained, but apparently nothing was done at the time . . .'.

The AFC's reply to this was a request for a copy of the clerk's first letter, sent in May 1918.

There is no record of payment having been made, so presumably the Australians still owe Tetbury Council £4 12s. 6d. (with interest!).

Fetching and carrying water in English winter conditions was not a favourite pastime of the Aussies. In December 1918 the AFC made a request to the town council for water connections to be made to their premises at Hampton Street and New Church Street, Tetbury. The council duly granted permission for the supply, but grudgingly insisted on it being metered, the device being installed outside the premises.

Sometime during February 1919, Tetbury lay under a thick blanket of snow; the first many of the Australians had ever seen.

Delight turned to despair when the water meter froze over and cut off the precious water supply, but they solved the problem in their own way. Later in the month the surveyor reported to the Town Clerk: '. . . the water meter on the Hampton Street premises occupied by the AFC has been completely destroyed through being set on fire when frozen. A new one to replace it will cost £4 7s. 6d.' The clerk was instructed to make a claim to the AFC and the surveyor told to get a new meter at once.

The minutes of the Town Council for April 1919 tell us that '. . . the Clerk was instructed to communicate again with the AFC with reference to the claim already sent out for the water meter in Hampton Street destroyed by them during the frost . . .'.

The AFC left for Australia in May 1919, leaving behind yet another unpaid bill.

Six AFC air mechanics make a snow kangaroo

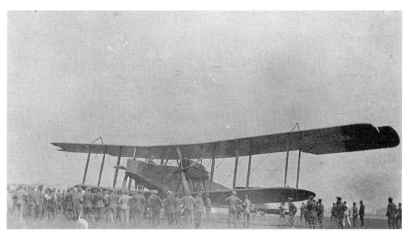

A huge Handley Page bomber causes great interest at Leighterton in 1918

97

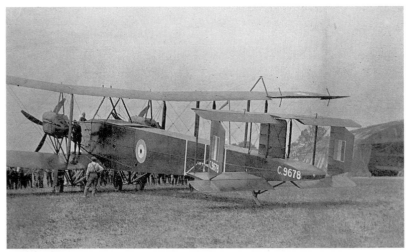

The Handley Page bomber, photographed by Jack Butcher

The Biggest Aeroplane in the World

Tales have been told that the biggest aeroplane in the world had been seen in the district and was based at Leighterton during the time of the AFC. Jack Butcher photographed this Handley Page bomber (which may well have been one of the biggest aeroplanes of its time) during its brief stay at Leighterton.

CHAPTER 7

The Leighterton Graves

Leighterton Cemetery is situated in the heart of the Gloucestershire countryside. In this beautiful setting lies the product of a wasteful war.

As the young fliers practised their turns and spins above the hills and valleys, they knew that the more proficient they became, the closer they were to being posted to the front where they would be lucky to live another fortnight. But training was also risky.

Despite Lt.-Col. Watt's obsession with safety, accidents were inevitable. The inexperience of the men, the crudeness of the machines and the opportunity for human error conspired to produce a large number of fatalities.

Not all the Australians who died were buried at Leighterton. At least seven more deaths were reported in the local press. Some of those killed had relatives in England who preferred to have the remains transported home, and there were others who had been so loved by those who had befriended them during their stay here that they were buried alongside local people in various churchyards.

There is one grave at Lasborough, probably because Lasborough House served as a temporary officers' mess, others at Tetbury and Cirencester. They are easily recognized, being standard War Graves Commission issue: white stone with a curved top.

An aerial view taken by the AFC of Lasborough House

One grave at Leighterton shows that Edward Baron Broomhall died in 1930. This was an AFC man who stayed on in the district after the war, working as a car salesman until his death from cancer. He had asked to be buried alongside his friends from the AFC.

The epitaphs found on some of the graves have a poignancy of their own. They express the desire of the relatives of those killed that the onlooker should know that their boys did not

'To live in hearts of those we love is not to die. Our Son, an Anzac'

die in vain, that they were doing their duty by volunteering to defend the Empire of which Australia was a part, and above all, that they were Anzacs and proud of it.

Though superbly kept and tended throughout the year the graves are at their best on the Sunday nearest Anzac Day when a special memorial service is held.

It begins with a parade down the narrow country lanes to the cemetery itself. A brass band leads the way through the wrought iron gates, followed by representatives of the Australian High Commission, the New Zealand High Commission and the RAAF. Local representatives might include Col. Lowsley-Williams from nearby Chavenage, or the Duke and Duchess of Beaufort, and always a large number of men, women and children from the surrounding district who come to pay their respects.

Anzac day at Leighterton, 1988

*The present-day ceremony is
organized by no. 2 Group, SW
Gloucestershire Royal British
Legion*

Over the years a number of visitors have made the journey from Australia to be present at the ceremony. Some worked here during the war, while others come to visit the graves of relatives. The visitors sign their names in a book at the nearby church where there is a roll of honour for the dead airmen.

The ceremony is organized by the Royal British Legion.

The very first memorial service at Leighterton was held at 10 a.m. on 17 November 1918. It was a much photographed event, no doubt for the benefit of relatives who could not be there:

Sunday the 17th was a memorable day in the annals of AFC Training Squadrons. A most impressive Memorial Service was held at Leighterton Cemetery where most of the Officers and Cadets killed in training are buried. At 10.00 a.m. a parade of 5, 6, 7 and 8 Squadrons and ARS

Leighterton, 17 November 1918

AFC cadets marching to the first memorial service at Leighterton,
November 1918

Staff officers motoring to the first memorial service at Leighterton,
November 1918

The service in progress. The central group is Oswald Watt, Col. Brinsmead and Maj. Browning

The first memorial service at Leighterton, 1918

under the command of Lt.-Col. Watt was held on the Leighterton Aerodrome and marched from there to the Cemetery about a mile distant. On a stand in the corner of the Cemetery well above the heads of the troops was the Padre, Major Norman. The troops were formed up in a hollow square around him as close as possible, the graves of the departed being in the centre. It was a cold dull day but in spite of the weather the service was most stirring and interesting. Upon the graves were wreaths of beautiful white and yellow flowers and the neat, well cut turf out of which mounds protruded made a picture of the ideal place for our Comrades' rest.

Sgt. Duigan, Temporarily Commanding 7th TS AFC

CHAPTER 8

Peace and Repatriation

Waiting to go Home

The end of the war in November 1918 did not mean the Australians' immediate repatriation. They had to wait another seven months for a troopship, the sailing date being set for 6 May 1919. Work was to continue till then at both aerodromes in order to strengthen the AFC and to relieve frustration brought on by boredom and homesickness. Maj. Phillips, Commander of 6th Squadron, remarked in his log for November 1918:

> The signing of the Armistice on Nov 11th upset the normal work of the Squadron, and dulled the keenness of both pupils and mechanics. Tact and discretion enabled us to regain the smooth running of work towards the end of the month.

In the build-up to departure many ceremonies took place, tokens were exchanged and a few sighs of relief were heard from both nationalities involved in the parting. Time had worked its magic on those who had been thrown together by the requirements of war. Many friendships had flourished and, now that the Australians were leaving, many a tear would be shed.

The atmosphere of impending departure had been building up since January when some local artistes from Dursley combined to give a concert for the men at Leighterton. The venue was the 'drome' itself. Some 200 officers and men enjoyed vocals from 'the Misses Ada Franklin, Margueritte Morgan and Trig'; Solos from E.R. Lewis, D. Price and Norman Rowles; a violin recital from Miss I. Boardman; and, intriguingly, 'Mrs S.G. Bennet was responsible for the humorous part of the programme.' (*Dursley Gazette*, 18 January 1919)

The Entertainments Committee at the Minchinhampton Aerodrome pulled out all the stops for a farewell concert at the Stroud Subscription Rooms. It was to be their best ever.

Coo-ee and Au Revoir
AUSTRALIA'S FAREWELL TO STROUD

Of all the good things the Australian airmen of the Minchinhampton aerodrome have provided for the delectation of Stroud appetites in the form of concerts, they undoubtedly kept the best in reserve for their farewell. The presence of the stalwart figures in the streets of our town and their nerve-wracking proximity to our chimney pots in their daring conquest of the Cotswold air, has given us an insight into the spirit of those of the far off land of sunny skies.

Stroud Journal

A specially prepared souvenir programme for the show declared: 'The memory of lavished kindness will bridge the distance that separates us.' During the interval there was a mad rush to exchange autographs between 'England's fair maidens and Australia's brave youths,' and then the scene was changed to a mock-up of the Minchinhampton aerodrome (see Chapter

3). This was capped by a specially written song, 'In the year 1921', which gave four of the airmen the opportunity to complain about the English weather and to hope for 'A little more sun' upon their intended return:

> The last scene was a delightful surprise. It was the embarkation for Australia of the boys now in their regulation khaki and picturesque hats. While waiting on the wharf there was more singing from the troops, and then one by one the boys took their places on board with their kit. When all were aboard coloured chains were thrown out from the ship and grasped by the audience, and amid wild enthusiasm the boat moved out from the pier, the troops singing with great gusto 'So long England'. When the troopship had passed from the stage the lights went out, and in the distance appeared the outline of a ship in fairy lamps while the song continued.
>
> *Stroud Journal*

Altogether, the Australian concerts had raised more than £500 for local and war charities.

Members of the Sergeants' Mess at Minchinhampton decided to organize a final fancy dress ball . . . with a difference:

FANCY DRESS BALL

BRILLIANT SCENE AT STROUD SUBSCRIPTION ROOMS

The great hall had been skilfully utilized for a display of the decorative art, and a prettier, more fascinating spectacle has rarely been seen in the West of England.

Stroud Journal

Centre-piece was a huge bell suspended from the ceiling with long strings of coloured streamers extending across the length of the room. The walls were decorated with flags and green foliage interspersed with coloured lights. There was a 'tip-top' band who played non-stop until between 4 and 5 a.m. the next morning. The highlight of the evening came at midnight:

. . . when the hour was struck the lights went out, and instantly flash lights at one end of the room were brought into play. The effect was striking and created plenty of amusement. The balcony was filled with spectators and these left the building more than ever impressed with the genius of the Australians.

Stroud Journal, 14 March 1919

Others found less public ways to express their gratitude to those locals who had shown kindness to them.

Mr and Mrs Mathews, the inadvertent receivers of the stolen pig (see Chapter 3), were presented with a silver tea and coffee service from their grateful colonial customers. The ladies who ran the canteen at the Corn Hall in Stroud, which served as an AFC club, were thanked at a farewell gathering and given a framed aerial photograph.

A Fond Farewell

An official goodbye was made to the town of Tetbury at the UDC meeting in April 1919:

PRESENTATION OF FLAG TO UDC

A deputation from the non-commissioned officers of the 1st Wing of the AFC attended the meeting, when Sergeant

The Corn Hall, Stroud, demolished during improvements to the town

Mechanic White acting on their behalf presented the council with their national flag and asked them to accept it as a mark of appreciation felt by himself and his comrades at the kind hearted manner in which they had all been treated during their stay and he also expressed a wish that the flag should be flown from the town hall on Anzac and Empire days. They had received nothing but kindness at the hands of all the townsfolk, while the ladies of Tetbury had been as mothers and sisters to them. In reply the Chairman (Mr Crow) said that a better lot of men had never come into the town (hear, hear) – and on every hand he had heard of the exemplary way in which members of the AFC had behaved. The old town had much to learn from the young Australians. They depended so much upon precedent and delved into musty documents to find out what happened a century before, while young Australians simply came to a decision on the facts before them. In conclusion he expressed the hope that friendships had been formed during the Australians' stay in the neighbourhood which would not easily be forgotten and that the flag would serve as a connecting link between them. (Applause)

The *Wiltshire and Gloucestershire Standard,* 26 April 1919

The flag was flown on the days specified for many years. Some time in the 1970s it mysteriously went missing. The Australian High Commission, when informed of this, responded by sending a special envoy to Tetbury with a replacement flag which now flies proudly on the flagpole of the parish church on the specified days.

On 27 March 1919 the *Dursley Gazette* reported that all the local workmen had been paid off. Local farmers heaved a sigh of relief. This was short-lived, however, as soon afterwards, farm labourers' wages were compulsorily raised from 30s. to 36s. 6d. per week.

During the April prior to sailing, most of the AFC personnel were given leave. Many had relatives in Great Britain
and took the opportunity to spend time with them. Others
tasted the delights of London. On 25 April a grand Anzac
Day parade was planned. The Prince of Wales, Gen.
Birdwood and Sir Douglas Haig would take the salute outside Australia House in the Strand. It was to be a grand
farewell to the Motherland and AFC pilots were given special permission to fly over London.

FAREWELL TO AUSTRALIANS

Red Devils flying 'stunts' astonish Prince of Wales

No doubt many of our readers read in the daily papers an
account of the Australian flying exhibition 'stunts' in
London on Anzac Day last weekend, when there was celebrated the fourth commemoration of the historic landing on
the bullet-swept beaches of Gallipoli, and the Prince of
Wales and Sir Douglas Haig took the salute of thousands of
marching Australians at Australia House, Strand.

During the march Australian airmen circled around, and
gave Londoners an exhibition of low altitude flying like
nothing seen in London before.

Stroud Journal, April 1919

Lt. Robertson of Minchinhampton aerodrome and Capt.
Cobby stationed at Leighterton took part in the fly-past which,
by all accounts, was the most dangerous aerial display ever
seen beneath the telegraph wires of London. Cobby freely

admitted that they were lucky to avoid a horrifying pile-up in the Strand, so close were the planes together.

On 1 May, Oswald Watt sent a final letter to the 'Inhabitants of the town and neighbourhood of Tetbury':

On the occasion of our departure from your midst, permit me to express on behalf of all the members of the Australian Flying Corps who have been working for the past fourteen months in Gloucestershire, our most sincere thanks for your never failing hospitality and courtesy. I feel sure that the opportunities we have all had of obtaining a glimpse of that home life, on the memory of which the foundations of the most distant settlements in the Empire have been so secure-ly based, cannot but help to draw yet closer those silken threads which bind us to the Homeland. On behalf of every one of us, I thank you.

It was suggested that the Australians might march through the town of Tetbury on the day of their departure but this idea was dismissed as the special train from Chalford Station was scheduled to depart for Southampton at 7 a.m. on 6 May. Nevertheless, they had no intention of leaving quietly.

Throughout Monday night there was a constant procession between the station and the billets of motor vehicles. Each journey was made to the accompaniment of vocal and instrumental music (?) – the performer on the cornet prov-ing himself to be a musician of no mean ability. We under-stand that the transport of the men from Leighterton to Tetbury was attended by a series of mishaps. It is reported that one motor tender encountered a flock of sheep being driven along the road at an early hour, with the unfortunate result that about a dozen of the animals were killed. Another tender appears to have collided with a second with sufficient force to set it on fire, resulting in its being abandoned as a total wreck by the roadside; while two other similar vehicles ran into each other, the occupants experiencing a miraculous escape.

The Wiltshire and Gloucestershire Standard, 10 May 1919

The next morning, at 5 a.m., 350 men and 35 officers marched from Minchinhampton aerodrome to Chalford station to the strains of an Australian piper. They were not allowed to leave unhonoured or unsung. Many hundred people from all parts assembled at Chalford railway station to bid them *au revoir* and *bon voyage*. Coffee, tea, biscuits, oranges, and

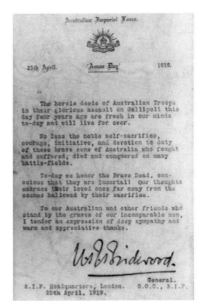

A letter of thanks from Gen. Birdwood to the Lowsley-Williams family

cigarettes were dispensed, and the train steamed out of the station at seven o'clock to the lusty cheers of the spectators and the answering cheers of the departing guests.

Bon Voyage

When they reached Southampton to board the SS *Kaiser-I-Hind,* the 1st Training Wing AFC were joined by the 2nd, 3rd and 4th Squadrons AFC from their camp on Salisbury Plain, the 1st Squadron having already returned home in March. Despite the cold, damp conditions on the day, many turned up to wave goodbye. Gen. (now Sir) William Birdwood stood alongside the mayor and corporation of Southampton surrounded by a brass band. Speeches were made from the specially constructed dais as the troops on board tried to throw

SS Kaiser-I-Hind: *the troopship that took the AFC home*

Officers and warrant officers aboard the Kaiser-I-Hind

oranges into the larger instruments being played by the band. The goodbyes lasted nearly two hours. As the boat moved off Australian songs were sung by all.

The voyage to Australia took six or seven weeks in those days, stopping off at various places *en route*. It was, by all accounts, a very pleasant journey.

They disembarked at Melbourne and returned to their towns and villages throughout Australia.

"1918" ANNUS MIRABILIS.

Entries in Alfred Taylor's autograph book, collected aboard the Kaiser-I-Hind, *June 1919*

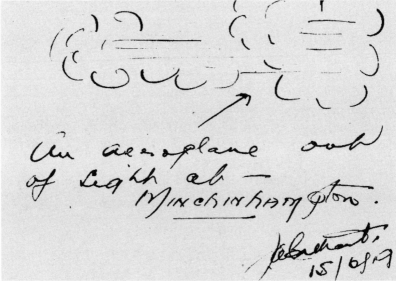

Fleas by night.
Flies by day;
Advance Australia
And scratch away.

> J. B. Fraser.
> Avenue Rd.
> Morman.
> N.S.W

Lives of great men
all remind us
We may make our lives sublime
and departing leave behind us
Footprints on the Sands of Time

> Sam. Fletcher
> Maylands W.A.

Officers, NCOs and men on board the Kaiser-I-Hind

CHAPTER 9

Left Behind: Men and Memories

Remaining Australians

Not all the Australians returned on the *Kaiser-I-Hind*. Those who had already married local girls, or intended to, were obliged to stay on and wait for a ship that could accommodate married couples.

Some chose to stay on for other reasons. Among these were the soldier-students.

In conjunction with the Australian Government, a scheme had been set up to allow some of the younger Australians to become students in engineering at the factory of R.A. Lister and Co. in Dursley. They were to be given instruction in Lister's Sheep Shearing Machinery Department.

So expert were they at using the machinery, that at a demonstration of Lister's machine at Tormarton in June 1919, two Australians sheared 540 sheep in twenty-one hours – a record at the time.

The spirit of goodwill lasted throughout the summer and the Australians left behind organized more social activities, such as dances and sports.

The most sensational story concerning the remaining Australians is of Capt. G.C. Mathews and his mechanic Sgt. T.D. Kay, who had been stationed at Minchinhampton aerodrome.

THE AUSTRALIAN STUDENTS OF
MESSRS. R. A. LISTER & Co.'s WORKS

have arranged for a

DANCE

to be held in

THE MESS ROOM

On WEDNESDAY, MAY 14th, 1919.

Tickets, to include Refreshments:—

LADIES, 2/-; GENTLEMEN, 2/6.

Admission by Ticket only.

Proceeds for the National Federation of Discharged Soldiers' and Sailors' Funds (Dursley Branch).

MUSIC SUPPLIED BY WORKS BAND.

FLYING TO AUSTRALIA.—Australian soldiers wishing good luck to Capt. G. C. Matthews, who started from Hounslow yesterday on his flight to Australia. In circle, Sergt. Kay, his mechanic. ["*Daily Mail.*"

A press cutting in the Chavenage presentation album

The Australian Government, noting the interest in the proposed England to America flight by Alcock and Brown, announced that it would offer £10,000 to the first Australian to fly from England to Australia. The first to make the attempt were Mathews and Kay.

On 21 October they left Hounslow aerodrome, flying a Sopwith Wallaby powered by a single 350 hp Rolls Royce Eagle engine. Capt. Mathews found time on the day of his departure to scribble a post office telegram to the Lowsley-Williams family at Chavenage, who had sent their good wishes for a safe journey:

MANY THANKS FOR MESSAGE. LEAVING TODAY.
REMEMBRANCE TO ALL. MATHEWS.

The journey was one of the most incredible in the history of flight and says a lot for the sheer courage and determination of the Australians. At one point, flying over Turkey at 13,000 ft with the temperature at -46 °F, the petrol pump seized up causing a forced landing in a field near Adrianole:

Sergeant Kay repaired the fault, but we could only get away by Kay hanging on the tail and making a flying jump for the fuselage at the take-off.

In Constantinople, preparing for the flight over Asia Minor, a leak was discovered in a water jacket. The search began for an acetylene welder to make the repair, but after ten days they could not find one:

With the aid of chewing gum, powdered asbestos, and copper wire, we repaired the leak, and set off on the 1,700 mile flight to Baghdad.

Forced to land again at Jansk near Bandar Abbas as one of the wings was broken:

We were then in the blazing desert under a scorching sun. We dragged it three miles to the shelter of an Englishman's verandah and there repaired it up again. The machine was then dragged back three miles to the Bandar Abbas aerodrome, and from there we reached Karachi in a non-stop flight.

At Bangkok, Sgt. Kay contracted dengue fever. He recovered

from this, but on 19 April 1920 the pair were forced to land at Bali in Java. During the landing both wings were smashed beyond recovery and the flight was abandoned before the last stage of the journey to Darwin.

Altogether, seven flights were attempted by Australian airmen from England. Several lost their lives in the attempt. The winners of the prize money were Capt. Ross Smith and his brother Lt. Keith Smith. With their navigators, Sgt. Bennet and Sgt. Sheers, they successfully landed their twin-engined Vickers Vimy at Darwin in the record time of just under 28 days. The distance covered was 11,340 miles and the actual flying time was 135 hours.

Remaining Buildings

Towards the end of 1919, notices appeared in local newspapers advertising the sale of second-hand building materials – the aerodromes were being dismantled.

Chief purchaser of the temporary Bessonaux Hangars was the firm of Chamberlains. They used them to house their press-board factory in Nailsworth on the site now occupied by a supermarket. The last of the hangars was removed in 1989.

For a short time, Leighterton aerodrome was occupied by 28th and 66th Squadron RAF, but both were disbanded by October 1919. In 1926 the site was purchased by builder John Herbert from Nympsfield, and the café he built, called the Aerodrome Café, is still operated by his daughter Mrs Maisie Martin. It is a popular meeting place for the sadly dwindling number of Australians who return to their old haunts. There is very little to see of the airfield buildings. Most of what remains lies covered with grass.

At Minchinhampton there are still many clues left pointing to the presence of the AFC. Some administrative buildings, half a brick-built hangar and the farm to which the aerodrome

By Direction of The Disposal Board.
LEIGHTERTON AERODROME.
BRUTON, KNOWLES & Co.
Are instructed to SELL BY AUCTION,
on WEDNESDAY AND THURSDAY,
JULY 9th and 10th, commencing each
day at 11.30 o'clock punctually,

SURPLUS BUILDING MATERIAL, 20
ARMSTRONG SECTIONAL HUTS,
and 3 NON-SECTIONAL HUTS, etc.
Catalogues may be had of the
Resident Engineer, Leighterton Aerodrome, or the Auctioneers, Albion Cham-
bers, Gloucester.

reverted after the war is now called 'Old Aerodrome Farm'. A
terrace of single-storey dwellings has the name of 'Old
Aerodrome Buildings'. Next to the old Australian site is Aston
Down Airfield, still used by the Ministry of Defence. The
Lowsley-Williams farmland, compulsorily purchased in 1917,
was repurchased and now a gliding school operates from there.

Among the photographs that survive is one taken by Capt.
Wrigley AFC. His inscription on the back solves the mystery
of the location of the Tetbury HQ.

Mr John Phillips in the Tetbury UDC meeting room, with an aerial photograph of Tetbury. On the back is written 'Birds eye view of Tetbury, Glos. taken by Capt. Wrigley. AFC in an Avro biplane with type L camera. Wing headquarters with red mark. My tent in ground marked red.' Capt. Wrigley was an instructor at Leighterton and went on to become Air Vice Marshall of the RAAF

Gordon House, Silver Street, Tetbury: 1st Wing AFC Headquarters

The remaining AFC buildings at Leighterton

The AFC aerodrome chapel at Minchinhampton, now a garden shed

The home of Mrs Margaret Chivers, originally part of the AFC living quarters at Minchinhampton, now a comfortable bungalow

The Aerodrome Café and Garage, Leighterton 1992, on the site of the AFC officers' mess

CHAPTER 10

The Anzac's Gloucestershire Diary

February 1918

Whist drive and dance at the Market House Minchinhampton to entertain AFC troops.

German prisoners held at Leighterton Camp.

March 1918

First sighting over Stroud of AFC aeroplanes being delivered from Shrewsbury.

Air raid on Stroud: AFC 'bomb' Stroud with leaflets in aid of funds to purchase aeroplanes.

Contractors advertising for tradesmen at both aerodromes.

Concert arranged by Miss Hawkins at Brimscombe for the AFC.

Ebley Glee Party gives a concert for the AFC.

Social Club opens at Leighterton for AFC.

Chipping Sodbury Farmers' Union resolution on wages.

Dance for AFC at Lister's Dursley women's canteen.

April 1918

Invitation whist drive at Market House Minchinhampton on Easter Monday to meet forty Australians from the aerodrome.

Anzac Day sports event at Leighterton aerodrome.

AFC football match at Fromehall Park.

Painswick accident, aeroplane written off, children hurt.

2nd Lt. Eric Duncan Grant killed in air crash at Minchinhampton: the first fatality.

Cadet George Needham killed in air crash at Leighterton.

May 1918

A rape involving an AFC man on Selsley Hill.

Boots stolen from Stroud by AFC men.

Warrant Officer Thomas Clutterbuck AFC dies of heart attack at George Hotel, Nailsworth.

Tetbury UDC requests stone to maintain roads to the aerodromes and increased petrol ration to bring extra water into the town.

June 1918

Bad flying weather until 20 June.

Short of aeroplanes, practice bombing raids on Leighterton aerodrome.

Thirty men and fourteen officers ill with influenza.

Officers' Mess opens on Minchinhampton aerodrome.

Sports committee formed: creditable Australian cricket team playing matches against local teams.

Three tennis courts made at Leighterton aerodrome: a Wing tennis championship started.

The Minchinhampton Station Concert Party puts on 'While the

Billy Boils' in Tetbury at the Empire Picture House in aid of Tetbury Hospital: £50 raised.

Water arrangements nearly completed: at present men have to walk two miles to Minchinhampton for a bath.

Garden fete at Burleigh Court including Australian whip cracking and concert party.

Social dance at the Stroud Subscription Rooms. 249 present.

'The Leighterton Resolution' tabled at Wotton-under-Edge UDC.

August 1918

Eight flying instructors now available at Leighterton, graduating from Instructors School at Gosport.

Fitters and riggers from all AFC flights being attached to 8th training squadron to gain experience on AVRO aircraft and rotary engines (Camel power units).

Aerial gunnery range chosen at Long Newton.

Officers' Mess moved from Lasborough House into newly built accommodation on the airfield on 15 August.

Cricket nets set up at Leighterton airfield.

Tennis tournament played off on the Leighterton Rectory court, by permission of the Revd W.E. Jackson: four tarmac courts being made on the airfield by the resident engineer.

Outside sports meetings held at Stroud, Dursley, Aldershot, Yatesbury and Wendover.

Exhibition boxing matches held at the YMCA hut in Leighterton and a proper ring and gymnasium planned for one of the 'stable huts'.

R.B. McCarthy of the AFC stole a bicycle in Stroud.

'The Welcome Nugget' performed by the AFC Concert Party in Stroud Subscription Rooms.

'Monster Procession' and Horticultural Show in Stroud includes a large contingent from the AFC.

Garden fête in Tetbury attended by many AFC officers and men.

Edward Fisher of Cashes Green knocked down at the top of Rowcroft, Stroud by motorcyclist Capt. Cornish of the AFC: Fisher dazed but able to walk home.

Killed in air crashes: 2nd Lt. O.D. Shepherd, Lt. R.A. Dunn, 2nd Lt. C.C. Lewis, Lt. S.C. Fry, 2nd Lt. R.L. Cummings, 1st Lt. C.W. Scott, 2nd Lt. E. H. Jefferys, Lt. H. Taylor MC, MM, Cadet Ferguson.

Died of appendicitis: 1st Air Mechanic L.G. Cubbins.

September 1918

Capt. Hall and Pte.Bray of AFC fined two shillings and sixpence in Nailsworth for driving a lorry dangerously.

Messrs Mytton, Patterson and Harden of AFC fined £1 18s. at Nailsworth for driving dangerously between Avening and Tetbury, knocking a young lady off her bicycle.

AFC members Lynas, Drain and Jay before magistrates for bicycle light offences.

Messrs Rose and Chesterman accused of stealing boots from the AFC.

Aquatic Gala at Stroud UDC Baths, AFC four-length championship: a magnificent race.

AFC Boxing Champions in Stroud: exhibition by Cadet Matty Smith, ex-Featherweight Champion of Australia.

AFC aeroplane forced landing at Stinchcombe Hill.

2nd Lt. W. Parks and Lt. Instructor P.G. Walsh killed in air crashes at Leighterton.

October 1918

Influenza rampant in Stroud district.

Dance and whist drive held in Stroud Subscription Rooms for AFC.

Improperly lit AFC lorry in Parsonage Street Dursley.

Impromptu concert for AFC men at YWCA in Dursley.

November 1918

First half of month ideal for flying instruction, but towards the end, much feared ground mists hang low for days over the aerodromes.

Signing of the Armistice upset the normal work of the squadron.

Nine pupils from Minchinhampton graduated and passed category 'B' by 30 November.

Memorial service held at Leighterton Cemetery attended by all officers and men of 5th, 6th, 7th and 8th squadrons under the command of Lt.-Col. Watt, 17 November.

Football match and Flying Kangaroo Concert Party at Wotton-under-Edge.

Rugby match, AFC vs Cheltenham College.

Premature Armistice celebrations in Stroud by AFC men and 'fair sex'.

Petrol ignited in Long Street, Tetbury, during Armistice celebrations by AFC.

AFC Concert Party at Amberley school to provide funds for a piano.

3rd AFC entertainment, 'Gee Whizz', performed at Stroud Subscription Rooms: proceeds for Christmas cheer for the wounded in Stroud and YMCA hut in France.

December 1918

'Flying Kangaroos' concert in Stroud in aid of the Red Cross.
'Flying Kangaroos' concert in Dursley.

January 1919

A 'Dinkum' concert at Stroud Subscription Rooms by the
Flying Kangaroos and the camp orchestra.
Return visit of the Flying Kangaroos to Dursley (R.A. Lister's
mess room).
Air accident at Leighterton: AFC Cadet fractures legs and ribs
but survives.
Water meter installed at Tetbury Hampton Street premises of
AFC.
Road accident at Barton End Nailsworth: 2nd Air Mechanic
F.G. Davis killed when he falls from a skidding AFC
lorry.
Concert given to AFC at Leighterton by local entertainers.
Pig stolen from Leighterton aerodrome.

February 1919

Six inches of snow falls: Water meter at Hampton Street,
Tetbury burnt by AFC to thaw water supply.
Miss Dorothy Woolford of Tetbury weds Air Mechanic W.A.R.
McVey AFC on 26 February.
Concert party from Minchinhampton aerodrome gives perfor-
mance at the Minchinhampton Market House in aid of funds
for town's war memorial.

Cadet C.C. Frederick AFC killed in air crash near Sapperton.
Lt. J.H. Weingarth AFC killed in air crash near Yate.
2nd Air Mechanics E.T. Filmer and R.N. McGuffie die of influenza and bronchitis at Tetbury Hospital.

March 1919

John King, farm labourer, charged with stealing cape from AFC's Leighterton stores.
Invitation dance held at Minchinhampton Market House for AFC.
Farewell fancy dress ball, 'Coo-ee and Au Revoir' held at Stroud Subscription Rooms.
Cadet T.L. Keen killed in air crash on last day of training.
Local workers at Leighterton aerodrome paid off on 27 March.
AFC officers supper for local friends held in Stroud Subscription Rooms: Lt.-Col. Watt present.
Minchinhampton aerodrome officially taken over by RAF.

April 1919

Australian flag presented to Tetbury town by AFC.
AFC pig larcenists committed for trial at Quarter Assizes.
Kenneth Knowlton AFC fined five shillings for riding a bicycle without lights in Nailsworth.
Norman Hall AFC summoned for dangerous driving at Box: case dismissed.

May 1919

Farewell party for AFC at Minchinhampton and Leighterton
held at AFC Club, Corn Hall, Stroud.
AFC leave the district 7 a.m., 6 May.
Departure of AFC from Southampton aboard *Kaiser-I-Hind*
troopship.

The AIF badge carved on a Leighterton gravestone

Australian Flying Corps Personnel buried at Leighterton

RANK	FULL NAMES	PLACE, COUNTRY OF BIRTH	LOCATION OF NEXT OF KIN ON ENLISTMENT
2 LT.(HON. LT.)	GEOFFREY DUNSTER ALLEN	NEWCASTLE,NSW	HABERFIELD,SYDNEY,NSW
1ST. AIR MECHANIC	SYDNEY HAROLD BANKS-SMITH	CUNDLETOWN (TAREE), NSW	TURRAMURRA,SYDNEY,NSW
2ND. AIR MECHANIC	EDWARD BARON BROOMHALL	BOX HILL, VIC.	DANDENONG. VIC.
1ST. AIR MECHANIC	HENRY BULAND	HAVRE, FRANCE	HAVRE, FRANCE
W.O.	THOMAS CLUTTERBUCK	BRISTOL,ENGLAND	SOUTH BRISBANE, QLD.
1ST. AIR MECHANIC	LINDSAY GORDON CUBBINS	ST. KILDA,VIC.	ST. KILDA, VIC.
2 LT.	ROY LYTTON CUMMINGS	SYDNEY, NSW	FRANKLIN, TASMANA
2ND. AIR MECHANIC	FRANCIS GORDON DAVIS	BALLARAT. VIC.	BALLARAT, VIC.
2 LT.	ROBERT ALEXANDER DUNN	NUMURKAH, VIC.	NUMURKAH, VIC.
2ND. AIR MECHANIC	EDGAR THOMAS FILMER	TRARALGON, VIC.	SARSFIELD,VIC.
2ND. AIR MECHANIC	CHARLES CLARENCE FREDERICK	SPOKANE, USA	PEKIN, CHINA
2 LT.	SYDNEY CHARLES FRY	MAITLAND,NSW	WEST MAITLAND, NSW
CPL (CADET)	ERNEST HOWARD JEFFERYS	LITHGOW, NSW	KURING-GAI, NSW
W.O.I.(CADET)	THOMAS LLEWELLYN KEEN (MC)	CANTERBURY, ENG.	DOVER, ENGLAND
2 LT.	CECIL CHARLES LEWIS	MANSFIELD. VIC.	MOYHU, VIC.
2ND.AIR MECHANIC	ROY NELSON VICTOR McGUFFIE	HOBART, TAS.	COOKTOWN, QLD.
2ND. AIR MECH.(CADET)	GEORGE FRANCIS JACK NEEDHAM	BUNA, SA.	ADELAIDE,SA.
2 LT.	WILLIAM PARKES	CRESWICK, VIC.	CRESWICK, VIC.
2ND.AIR MECH.(CADET)	ROY NELSON PILLOW	GEELONG, VIC.	GEELONG, VIC.
LT.	CHARLES WILLIAM SCOTT	MALVERN, VIC.	NORTH CARLTON,VIC.
2 LT.	OSCAR DUDLEY SHEPHERD	GOULBURN,NSW	GOULBURN, NSW
2ND.AIR MECH.(CADET)	KEITH WILLIAM STRONACH	MELBOURNE,VIC.	PERTH, WA
LT.	GEORGE ROBERT THOMPSON	S. MELBOURNE,VIC.	ST. KILDA, VIC.
LT.	PATRICK GEORGE WALSH	CUNNAMULLA,QLD.	TOOWOOMBA, QLD.
LT.	JACK HENRY WEINGARTH	MARRICKVILLE,NSW	DARLING POINT, NSW

140

PLACE OF ENLISTMENT	DATE OF DEATH	NEXT OF KIN & LAST KNOWN ADDRESS
SYDNEY, NSW	7 SEP. 1918	FATHER-GEORGE ALLEN, 7 DEAKIN AVE., HABERFIELD, NSW (MARCH 1932)
QUEEN'S PARK, NSW	3 JULY 1918	MOTHER -FLORENCE LODGE, LAST KNOWN AT: NELSON ST. GORDON, NSW, BUT UNTRACEABLE IN 1929.
DANDENONG, VIC.	9 MAY 1930	FATHER - L.F. BROOMHALL, BOX 1307 GPO MELBOURNE (DECEMBER 1918)
GUILDFORD, WA	10 FEB. 1919	BROTHER- LEON JOSEPH SENATEUR BULAND (FEB. 1926) 43 RUE AUGUSTE COMTE, LE HAVRE, FRANCE.
SYDNEY, NSW	22 MAY 1918	WIDOW- MRS A.F. CLUTTERBUCK, AMELIA ST. BURANDA, SOUTH BRISBANE (AUGUST 1923)
MELBOURNE, VIC.	14 AUG. 1918	FATHER - MR JAMES CUBBINS 'AILSA', 24 JOHN ST., ST. KILDA SOUTH, VIC. (DECEMBER 1918)
CLAREMONT, TAS.	28 AUG. 1918	FATHER - DR. HAROLD LYTTON CUMMINGS, FRANKLIN, TASMANIA (JULY 1921)
BALLARAT, VIC.	25 JAN. 1919	FATHER - MR. A.E. DAVIS, NORTH LODGE, WENDOUREE PARADE, BALLARAT WEST, VIC. (MAY 1919)
MELBOURNE, VIC.	13 AUG. 1918	MOTHER - MRS. A. DUNN, NUMURKAH, VICTORIA (DECEMBER 1922)
SALE, VIC.	12 FEB. 1919	FATHER - EDGAR S. FILMER, SARSFIELD, GIPPSLAND, VICTORIA (OCTOBER 1922)
MELBOURNE, VIC.	4 FEB. 1919	BROTHER - MR. O.A. FREDERICK, 41 FOLEY ST., KEW VICTORIA (JUNE 1921)
LIVERPOOL, NSW	24 AUG. 1918	FATHER- MR. H.W. FRY, 3 MICHAEL ST., WEST MAITLAND NSW (FEBRUARY 1919)
SYDNEY, NSW	28 AUG. 1918	FATHER- MR. P. JEFFERYS, RAILWAY STATION, KURING-GAI, NSW (JUNE 1919)
LIVERPOOL, NSW	12 MAR. 1919	MOTHER- MRS T.B. KEEN, 57 HEATHFIELD AVE., DOVER, ENGLAND (MARCH 1919)
MELBOURNE, VIC.	14 AUG. 1918	FATHER -JOSEPH LEWIS, 'THISTLEBROOK" MOYHU, VICTORIA (APRIL 1923)
TOWNSVILLE, QLD.	19 FEB. 1919	WIDOW- LUCY VERONICA SEAGREN (NEE McGUFFIE) ADDRESS UNKNOWN AFTER RE-MARRIAGE
ADELAIDE, SA	23 APR. 1918	BROTHER - MR. R.W. NEEDHAM, MORNINGTON, PALMER PLACE, NORTH ADELAIDE, SA, (NOVEMBER 1922)
ADELAIDE, SA	1 SEP. 1918	MOTHER - SELENA PARKES, CLUNES RD., CRESWICK, VICTORIA (SEPTEMBER 1920)
MELBOURNE, VIC.	24 AUG. 1918	FATHER -HENRY PILLOW, 'MINERVA', LAUREL BANK PARADE, GEELONG, VICTORIA, (APRIL 1923)
MELBOURNE, VIC.	28 AUG. 1918	MOTHER- MRS. AGNES A. SCOTT, 507 LYGON ST., NORTH CARLTON, VICTORIA (JANUARY 1922)
SYDNEY, NSW	11 AUG. 1918	FATHER - FREDERICK SHEPHERD, TENERIFFE', GOULBURN NSW. (APRIL 1919)
BRISBANE, QLD.	7 JULY 1918	FATHER - SAMUEL WILLIAM STRONACH, 1048 HAY ST. PERTH, WA. (DECEMBER 1918)
MELBOURNE? VIC.	3 JULY 1918	WIDOW- MRS. M.L. THOMPSON, 'VACUNA - FAULKNER ST., ST. KILDA, VICTORIA, (SEPT. 1919)
TOOWOOMBA, QLD.	30 SEP. 1918	FATHER - RICHARD WALSH, GOODWOOD, GOODWOOD ST. NEWTOWN, TOOWOOMBA, QLD. (FEB. 1923)
SYDNEY, NSW	4 FEB. 1919	NEPHEW- MR. G.F. WEINGARTH, SYDNEY, NEW SOUTH WALES

141